Th

Diamond

Light

Messages from the Ascended Master
Djwhal Khul
for the 21st Century

Violet Starre

woke up to Walking on the Moon on ttd moon

Some day! wishing my days away No way.

Light Technology Publishing

Cover art by Delmary

ISBN 1-891824-25-2

Published by
Light Technology Publishing
P.O. Box 3540
Flagstaff, AZ 86003

About Djwhal Khul

Ascended Master
Djwhal Khul

Master Djwhal Khul is mostly known for the books produced through the telepathic channelings of Alice A. Bailey. She was a Theosophist who founded the Arcane School and the Lucis Trust, which published roughly 26 books between 1919 and 1949. At the time of her first contact with Djwhal Khul, he presided over a Tibetan monastery, still incarnate in a human body, and referred to himself as an elder brother to humanity. During the period of his involvement with Alice Bailey he ascended to become one of the newer masters and works very closely with the Master Kuthumi.

Since Bailey's death, the Master Djwhal Khul has worked through a variety of channels, including Dr. Joshua Stone, Terri Sue Stone, Janet McClure and several others, and there will probably be more in the future. As he has expressed the thought to me, he has become rigidly identified with Alice Bailey and wishes to broaden the general perception of his identity by working through many different channels.

He is part of the planetary council of Ascended Masters, which consists of spiritual beings who attained this level of consciousness through differing spiritual paths over many lifetimes — Christianity, Hinduism, Buddhism, Islam and other religions — but who all share a certain common level of compassion, humility and enlightenment. He is on the ray of Love/Wisdom, which is to say that he is one of the main planetary entry points for this energy, and his main focus is teaching.

Contents

Foreword

The purpose of this book is to present esoteric teachings similar to those given to Alice A. Bailey during the period between the two great world wars and offer them to the public in an updated form that is short, concise and simple. The original teachings from the Master Djwhal Khul were presented in lengthy volumes that were somewhat difficult to understand without a thorough background in the religion known as Theosophy, founded by Madame Blavatsky in the late 19th century. It is the Master's current wish that he contribute a short book to the world that is simple and clear to the general New Age reader.

The Master is one member of a planetary council of spiritual beings who exist within another dimension and who guide the spiritual destiny of this planet and the life forms on it. Although a spiritual government exists, it does not interfere with the free will of humanity but occasionally sends teachers to guide us.

It should also be noted that I, the channel, am not a teacher who presents lectures, workshops and tapes, but a most ordinary person. The Master would like to convey the concept that he is accessible to average mortals and does not reserve his communication only for the most well-read and well-known advanced souls. Rather, he is available for those who most desperately need him, who feel as if they are struggling to survive in the modern world without a message of hope. I do not own any of the Alice Bailey books, nor have I found them in my local library. I have not read any of them for more than twenty years. I am trying to maintain an occupation that has little to do with the world of spiritual teachers. This book was not written by me, so I do not wish to be given credit for it. I am a person of humble means without worldly status.

I can honestly say that it was never my ambition to become a channel. I never held channels in awe. I read their messages with open-minded interest and evaluated the content rather than the source.

The most well-known channels usually go into a trance state and their spoken words must be transcribed. I am not a trance channel; I receive a stream of ideas that are clothed in words in my subconscious mind. This process began for me in November 1997. While meditating, I mentally reached out to contact the Master Djwhal Khul. I had never attempted to do such a thing before, but this action was prompted because in the far past I had studied some of the Alice Bailey books and was perplexed about a criticism of them that I had stumbled upon on an Internet Web page. Much to my surprise, an immediate stream of thoughts flowed into my head. In other words, my mind was relatively blank except for the usual worries — then suddenly it was full of thoughts.

In theosophical books, the authors had always warned the student on the spiritual path never to bother the busy masters, who are always working on carrying out the details of the divine plan and are not interested in the problems of the lowly student.

The immediate response I got that day was that the Master Djwhal Khul exists outside of time; he assured me that he has an infinite amount of time, thus his time cannot be wasted. I had always thought it took a special kind of person, a psychic person, to be a channel. What I learned is that many have the capacity to do this, but generally speaking, people do not wish to do so.

There are several reasons that people do not wish to channel, and one reason is that channeling sounds a lot like the clinical definition of mental illness and psychosis, of hearing voices in one's head or having delusions of thought insertion. Thought insertion (the idea that one's thoughts are not one's own) is a major preoccupation in some forms of mental illness. So I had to give the matter a great deal of thought in order to be clear about how telepathic channeling differs from psychosis. I came to several conclusions.

The first conclusion is that mentally ill people do not know that the voices are in their heads. They hear voices as if people were in the room with them. This is very frightening to them and very real. It is an auditory hallucination. Those we call channels do not hear voices. The second point is that those in a state of psychosis have no control over this phenomenon and cannot consciously stop it. The third is that the thought content is never lucid and coherent, but disjointed and chaotic.

Another fear is that one might open up to some form of possession by an evil spirit or a mischievous prankster.

I think the key here is to protect oneself in meditation by invoking white light and one's own higher self and to (this is very important) mentally specify the name of the entity one wishes to communicate with. By consciously seeking to connect with a specific being, the danger of tuning in to some other being is reduced. I think it is also important to try to live a decent lifestyle and be the best person one can be.

Another fear is that most of the information might

be coming from one's own subconscious and is of no value. I have struggled with this idea myself, and I cannot get absolute proof that there really is a Master Djwhal Khul even though I have asked the Master for proof that he is real. To the best of my understanding, I have to make a leap of faith, because conclusive proof would interfere with my free will. I have come to the conclusion that these teachings are useful no matter what the source.

However, what I have experienced since I started channeling and writing down these teachings is a total change in my viewpoint about reality. Of course, this might be an unhealthy situation that would indicate I am becoming mentally unstable. But it would be more accurate to say that *before* this experience, my normal state of being, with its constant fearfulness, worry and sense of being alone, was closer to mental imbalance than when I was channeling this book.

Some people who know that I do this expect me to behave with the love, wisdom and compassion of a master, but of course there is no reason why I should, since I am not as evolved as the Master. However, I have learned many concepts in this process. Certainly I am familiar with some of the information that comes through, but there are small pieces of totally new information that bind it together for me.

The Image of the Blue-White Diamond

Early on in my contact with the Master, he gave me an image to meditate on. It was the image of a many-faceted diamond suspended in space and radiating blue-white light. It is a very potent image. Over the months, I spent a lot of time meditating on it. I looked up the symbol of the diamond from other authors and teachers, but much of its significance came through books and meditations.

The diamond is a symbol of the human soul and of the initiate. It is formed from carbon under extreme pressures deep in the Earth and must be cut and polished to reveal its clarity and beauty. Likewise, the human soul journeys through many lifetimes to be cut and polished by life until the beauty of its core stands revealed.

The diamond symbolizes the completion of the soul's journey. I take it to be a symbol of a master. Thus it came as quite a surprise to me when I recently looked up Tibetan Buddhism and learned that this form of Buddhism is sometimes called the Diamond Way.

In the earliest contact with Djwhal Khul I found that all my conceptions about masters were changed by his presence. He often interjects humor. He is nothing but loving, for it is not within his nature to be critical or to find fault. This may be hard to understand for those readers who imagine that the spiritual teacher always finds imperfection, scolds, condemns and urges the student to try harder or do better in an impersonal fashion. But this is apparently not within the consciousness of Master Djwhal, who knows and understands much more than we can comprehend. His method is to teach and enlighten with mental models and concepts that change the consciousness of the student. The word "discernment" is frequently used by him in reference to many situations. He frequently emphasizes that free will cannot be violated and that the individual must ask for help. The individual must ask for contact with a master and not sit around waiting for a teacher to appear.

The next step forward for those who have been meandering along the path of metaphysics and meditating, visualizing, reading New Age books and attending workshops and seminars is to make contact with the teacher within. The inner teacher may not necessarily be an ascended master, but an entity who works specifically with that individual.

The teacher within can give specific training that matches the stage along the path that the aspirant has reached. Many would probably wonder why a teaching guide should be contacted rather than the higher self. I personally have simply found it easier to contact the Master than to contact my higher self. My higher self seems to communicate more along the lines of hunches and intuitions than teachings.

The overall theme that unites the chapters of this book is the general escalation of the spiritual energies that are now entering this planet. There may be some inaccuracies where my consciousness and my biases have superimposed themselves over the thoughts transmitted by the Master. This is somewhat inevitable in the telepathic channeling process.

I would also like to explain to the general reader that I personally believe that I have known the Master Djwhal Khul in many past lives and that many of my past lives had oriental and monastic settings. I also believe we have a good rapport, which makes it possible for me to make a strong connection with him. This is not because I am as spiritually evolved as he is — far from it — but because we are part of the same karmic group of souls.

— Violet Starre, 1998

Introduction by Djwhal Khul

Perhaps you are standing in a bookstore thumbing through the pages of this little book, wondering if this book contains the insights you are looking for. Perhaps you are wondering who the Ascended Master Djwhal Khul is and whether he really exists or ever did. Ultimately, it does not matter who the source is, but whether the contents are enlightening and useful to you and whether, after reading this book, you can understand more metaphysics and the significance of the present time in Earth history.

My perspective is that of one who has been a Tibetan Buddhist monk who eventually presided over a monastery. In that life I focused on meditation, contemplation, study, simple chores and training and teaching younger monks. This life culminated many others spent in the monasteries of the Orient and in more mundane activities. The contemplative life makes it possible to raise consciousness to higher levels, and it is a testing ground to see how well one has learned the principles one has studied.

The goals of my Tibetan incarnation were to attain my true Buddha nature, demonstrate my compassion for all sentient beings, break free of the bonds of reincarnation and join the Noble Ones. Thus I am writing this book as one who has attained these goals and who now dwells in what might be considered a different dimension. Or I might be referred to as a mind without a body! At the time when I transcended to a higher level, I gained insights into a greater realm of knowledge and wisdom than had been available to me as a man incarnated on Earth. So I am not writing from the perspective of a Buddhist, but from that of one of the spiritual hierarchy who guides the life on this planet.

My partner in this venture has asked me what has made me a master while she is not. She asks what the defining qualities and virtues are that have earned me the status of master and why there are so few of us on the planet. She wonders why there are not millions of masters.

First, this planetary school has indeed produced thousands of masters over thousands of years, but very few have taken the bodhisattva vow to remain on this planet and work with a suffering humanity. What is especially noteworthy about this particular time in Earth history is that many of these masters from the Earth school are coming back to the planet to assist in the changes taking place.

The second part of her question was to ask what special virtues and acts have made me a master. As ever, the term "master" indicates that I have gained total mastery over myself through many lifetimes of effort. This means that I have managed to impose the higher will of my higher self on every aspect of my lower nature. Left to its own devices, my lower nature was like an animal that needed to come under the control of my higher will, and I wrestled with the usual human frailties such as laziness, avarice, greed, anger, lust, dishonesty, fear, worry and violence over the span of many lifetimes. I did not learn to control my nature in a repressive fashion, such as many use to hide their rage to appear free of anger, for example. Rather, I gradually learned a state of viewing reality that made such emotions irrelevant from a broader perspective.

So, I am master over myself and no one else, and I

do not impose my will on others or tell them what they should be doing with their lives. The road to self-mastery took the form of a never-ending series of tests of my character and skills to see whether I had integrated my understanding to the point where I could be trusted with the power of a master, and many of these tests determined whether I was selfless and compassionate toward the sufferings of others and, of course, never caused suffering to others in my later lives.

It is easy to maintain a demeanor of selflessness and calm if one is never in a situation that tests these qualities to the maximum, and the final test given to me was difficult in the extreme.

While I was a monk in Tibet, I made telepathic contact with my own master as I progressed. I was aware of the Theosophical movement and was eventually given the assignment of working telepathically with Alice Bailey. This process of collaboration was to some extent intended to be a growing and broadening experience for both of us, as we were exactly opposite in background and training. She had a strong background in Christian mysticism and theosophy and had been a member of the Theosophical Society. My background was from living many lifetimes in the oriental traditions of Taoism, Hinduism, Buddhism and other lesser known Eastern traditions. The resulting collaboration between myself and Alice Bailey produced works that were predominantly Christian and theosophical in flavor, with a heavy emphasis on self-abnegation and selfless service. They were, to a large extent, written for and aimed at the membership of the Arcane School. This little book is in no way intended to be a treatise, nor is it intended to mimic the style of Alice Bailey, for she did indeed have her own language style. This work is intended to be a key to open intuitive doors of perception for the reader and tie together differing schools of esoteric thought with the newer materials being channeled and published.

Part of what I am attempting to accomplish at this time, in coordination with all the other teachers on the inner planes, is to present information in new terminology, moving away from some of the terms that came into use at the end of the last century. One clear example would be the ubiquitous use of the term "White Brotherhood." This was the translation of the concept of an intergalactic group of human souls bound together by spiritual purpose and alignment to the divine will by a level of embodiment of this divine purpose and by a personal spiritual interconnectedness.

But this term has gender and race implications we never desired, ones that conjure images of white-haired, white-robed white males united in some elitist fraternity. The thought behind these words more correctly corresponds with the words "Family of Light," or "Light Family," and you may notice this term creeping into the newer channeled teachings.

The Family of Light is the White Brotherhood, but these newer words have a much broader and more inclusive scope. Also, at this time the Family of Light is gathering on this planet from locations all over the galaxy. It includes members of the Family from such exotic locations as the Pleiades, Arcturus, Sirius and other star systems. All these members of the Family of Light are principally here on the inner dimensions and not physically present in tangible spaceships. These members of the intergalactic Family of Light are ancient and wise teachers who work in cooperation with the planetary council to promote the spiritual evolution of this planet. They have asked to be allowed to work through various channels to dispense teachings to the masses. My present interest is to form a bridge between the work begun by the planetary hierarchy at the end of the last century and the newer teachings coming at this time.

The work I undertook with Alice Bailey was aimed at a specific group of people who thought of themselves as disciples. I would like to move away from this term and all that it implies. This particular word has a certain elevated quality to it, but there are also strong associations with the disciples of Jesus, of Christian mysticism, of being a follower and of obeying the dictates of an authority other than oneself. Rather than use the term "disciple," I would prefer to use the word "lightworker," which suggests an independent being whose nature is light and whose activities and work must therefore be in the nature of light.

You may be starting to understand that much of the work initiated more than seventy years ago became tainted by the usage of certain terms and that we who began these projects had to go back to the drawing board and restrategize the presentation of our teachings to a modern readership as well as employ the assistance of beings from other star systems.

Another example of an obviously unfortunate word is the term "master," which implies a male who dominates and owns others and which often has the initial effect of causing those unfamiliar with the concept of the ascended masters to recoil in horror and declare their refusal to follow the dictates of *any* master. Of course, in reality and on an intergalactic level, a master is a soul who has complete mastery over those parts of self that incarnate into matter, and there are countless masters who may be conceptualized as *both* male and female. The masters exist at a particular dimensional level of reality — that of the higher mental plane — but they can choose to appear or not on the physical level. We have not come up with an excellent word to substitute for the term "master," but perhaps the term "game master" gives a better sense of an individual who has become an expert in utilizing the rules of the universe and developing personal skills toward reaching a certain level in a cosmic game.

One of the last tasks that Alice Bailey and I undertook together was meditation work, using the Great Invocation within a large group of Arcane School members to energize the etheric grid of light. This was a tremendous venture, and it has been very successful due to the tireless work of the members of the Arcane School and the Lucis Trust as well as those they influenced over the past fifty years or so. We have reached a point now where lightworkers meditating all over the planet act as anchor points for this grid, and it is now possible for the planetary hierarchy to send carefully planned pulses of cosmic energies through this grid, energies that are accelerating the planetary being along the path of return on the evolutionary arc, as well as accelerating everything else on the planet.

What we are trying to do here is give something of an update on what has transpired since Alice Bailey completed her task, because some of what was taught in those books has become outdated and is no longer relevant. Although some of it still holds true, world conditions have changed a great deal in the fifty-two years or so that have passed since Alice Bailey last wrote.

So this little book is an attempt to catch up on the

turn of events since the end of World War II. Obviously, the group of masters described by Alice Bailey has been working consistently since then with the most promising students in all fields of endeavor, and changes have been occurring on the inner planes as well. I am part of a small team of spiritual beings who form a governing council concerned with the spiritual direction of the Earth. During this century great numbers of the Family of Light from other star systems have requested to come to this planet and assist with its transformation. They do this in a number of ways, but principally by anchoring energies here. A massive team of lightworkers is gathering in the fifth dimension to help us speed up the evolution of the planetary being.

Changes are taking place by leaps and bounds in the consciousness of humanity. There was a time when books such as this could be found only in the most obscure bookstores in the largest cities. This is no longer true. The interest in and demand for metaphysical books can be found in some of the smallest rural communities.

As we pass the end of the twentieth century — a century of turmoil and tremendous technological advance — there is a strong sense that something really important is going to occur. What transpires will be a reflection of the consciousness of humanity as a whole and of the ability of the race to align itself with these incoming energies that will have many specific effects. Some of these effects include the emergence of telepathic communication between individuals; an increased ability to penetrate the veil and contact angels, guides, masters and other entities in meditation; the certain knowledge that thoughts create reality; and an increase in the numbers of those who become conscious on the astral plane in their dream state.

We are looking at a very exciting decade before us, and the speed at which these events take place will depend on the mass consciousness of humanity as well as the extent to which humans can move forward in awareness, rejecting all forms of elitism, separatism, hatred and violence and embracing those causes that promote peace, unity, equality, human rights and planetary healing in all forms.

1

Into the Millennium and Beyond

I would like to address some topics that have not been emphasized in the wealth of channeled materials being released at this time. This is a momentous time in Earth history, with many events converging. Many viewpoints are being offered as to the significance of the millennium and the years immediately following, to the end of the Mayan calendar in 2012. Some individuals are promoting concepts taken from the Bible and the predictions of Nostradamus, while others are teaching that it will be a time of catastrophes and Earth cleansing. Others are telling you that we are approaching a time when the Earth is going through a major transition toward a higher level of vibration, caused by an influx of cosmic energies that will bring the planet to a higher frequency. I am writing from the latter perspective as being closes to the truth. This beautiful planetary being is transitioning to a new and higher level, which I will refer to as the fourth dimension. A golden age is approaching — a new age.

Many of you would like to believe in the beautiful ideals presented through channels, but your rational, skeptical minds are confounded by the frequent use of such jargon as *energies, frequencies* and *vibrations*. You may feel that these concepts are too vague and unscientific and that modern science has somehow proved that nothing exists beyond the physical realm — therefore, there are no such beings as disembodied spirits who might dispense information through channels.

In the late 1800s, your forebears were riding in horse-drawn carriages and reading by gaslight, and our theosophical students were teaching that the universe is constructed of atoms. From my perspective as one of the elder brothers associated with the masters involved in dispensing the ancient wisdom teachings to the public at that time, the general mood of skepticism at present strikes me as not only highly ironic, but the inevitable result of brief life spans and short memories.

Back in the late 1800s nobody really believed in the existence of atoms, and many laughed at our teachings. We generally advise our students to be skeptical and to always use discernment, but not to dismiss the ancient mystery teachings in their new form without due examination. The ancient Greeks were familiar with the concept of atoms, which they in turn learned about from even earlier sources kept in the great libraries of the ancient world. These were later destroyed by barbarian hordes. Is it not astounding that these people who lived without the benefit of the electron microscope wrote extensively on the topic of atoms? The ancient wisdom teachings as presented by the early theosophists are entirely based on an understanding of atomic physics that far exceeds the understanding of modern science — still in its infancy compared to the wonders that lie in the future.

You know that the manifest universe as you view it is entirely composed of atoms and that these atoms are constructed of a central nucleus and electrons that orbit around the nucleus at tremendous speeds. It is the speed at which electrons orbit around the nucleus that defines what we call the various dimensions of the universe. The electrons of your third-dimensional reality move relatively slowly, therefore your reality is described as dense, slow or low in vibration. The speed of light is a limit or boundary to your reality, since any object — whether electron, atom, molecule or groups of atoms and molecules — that moves faster than the speed of light would disappear from your sight. This does not mean that the object would cease to exist, but that you would cease to *perceive* it. It would have crossed over the boundary into the next dimension. Thus the higher dimensions are composed of atoms, just as this dimension is. But these are atoms whose electrons move at speeds that are faster than light.

You might ask then what the esotericist means by energy. When a physicist talks about energy, he or she is generally referring to the release of heat, radiation, light or electricity through a chemical that releases the bond between the nucleus and its electrons. Energy usually moves from its source in a linear fashion, sometimes in waves. It usually consists of subatomic particles.

From the esoteric point of view, energies are fast-moving particles directed by the power of thought from higher dimensions and at speeds that are faster than light.

Now you begin to get a sense that your reality is all movement — from the small circular movements of electrons to the linear movement of energy. What remain relatively still or fixed, in a universe that is never still, are the nuclei of atoms. Clearly, this is a vast oversimplification of a very complex topic, but I wish to have you pause and contemplate the continuous rapid movement of atoms and energies that create the illusion of your known reality.

I want to interject at this point that we who teach through channels currently prefer the term "dimension" to "plane" because it is a modern term that has emerged largely out of science fiction writing. Many of you can easily relate to this through your current books and movies. The older theosophical teachings released at the end of the last century and other occult literature, such as the writings from the Order of the Golden Dawn, clearly delineated other realities in terms of *planes*. The physical plane is, in esoteric thought, composed of five elements: Earth, air, fire, water and ether — ether being a finer element than gas. Ether exists at the top end of the scale of the physical plane. I will often refer to the physical plane as the third dimension.

The dimension closest to the physical plane is the astral plane, of which there are seven levels and infinite locations. These are frequently referred to as the fourth dimension.

The next plane above the astral has been referred to as the mental plane, which consists of seven levels, the lower levels having been referred to as concrete, the upper levels as abstract. We now refer to the mental planes as the fifth dimension. Most of the teachers who are working through channels are located on the abstract mental plane — the higher levels of the mental plane or fifth dimension.

In science fiction, characters are able to move from one dimension to another. But this is not exactly the case, since you are already in all dimensions; only your *consciousness* is limited to the third. Everything you perceive in your third- dimensional reality has energy matrices in the fourth, fifth, sixth and higher dimensions that help to hold your physical form together.

There has been much progress in your scientific technology related to working with sound vibrations and using the higher frequencies, but do not confuse the principles of sound with energy. Sound is vibrations through atoms, usually gases. Sound moves the atoms in wave formations, some of which are so fast that they are well above the audible range of humans. They are nevertheless contained within the third dimension because sound depends on the atoms of gases.

Science has presented a picture of reality that eliminates any phenomena that cannot be examined by the five senses, but it has succeeded in extending the five senses only by magnifying vision and hearing through technological devices. By extending vision, science has learned of emanations from the Sun and other sources that you cannot sense, see, hear or touch, such as ultraviolet rays. I suggest that there are entire dimensions of reality that science cannot register in any measure because they are completely outside the range of the five senses; hence science must be forever limited.

In the esoteric teachings we present a cosmology based on seven planes with seven subplanes, all of which are composed of frequencies of atoms that range in octaves like a keyboard instrument. So, holding the image of a keyboard, the physical plane might be likened to the frequency or tone of the lowest C and octave, and ranging above it are dimensions that correspond to the remaining octaves, becoming higher and higher in frequency. You might ask what I mean by the frequency of atoms. I would answer that for the sake of simplicity, I mean the speed at which the electrons move around the nucleus of the atom, which on the physical plane is relatively slow.

Having attempted to define the esoteric view of the nature of reality, wherein there is no division of matter and spirit but rather an endless vista of higher and higher- frequency atoms, the question must arise: What is consciousness? Again, from the esoteric view, we are conceptualizing All That Is, Source or the Supreme Being as a vast ocean of consciousness, the source of all consciousness that imbues creation with Itself, consciousness. We might attempt to define consciousness as the sense that I Am. Therefore, the journey each individual spark of consciousness takes will go deeper and deeper into the dimensions of matter, then return through the higher dimensions to the Source.

So the process by which your planet is raised to the fourth dimension involves the application of energies from higher dimensions, which are streams of infinitely small particles moving faster than the speed of light that cause the electrons to accelerate, just as heat causes atoms to increase their activity.

Simultaneous to the increase in your world's electronic frequency, which is being induced by surges of energy through the etheric grid of your planet, major changes are taking place in the fourth dimension. One of the functions of the fourth dimension is that of a sort of holding tank for souls who have passed over in death to the next dimension. This is possible because all living forms in the third dimension have an electrical matrix in the fourth that holds their form together, so to speak. The lowest and slowest vibrational level of the fourth dimension holds souls who have a very low, selfish, destructive level of consciousness. As the two worlds rapidly approach each other, the souls on these lower levels are being transported through special energy portals to another planet in order to start a new planetary round. This is not a negative occurrence in any sense, as these souls will gain a new opportunity to progress in a new world. However, they will not be able to hamper the progress of souls in this world. As this process gradually takes place, you will notice a decrease in violence and ill will in your world.

Those of you who are familiar with the theosophical teachings may have gained the impression that only a few souls from the human evolutionary chain have attained the highest levels of consciousness and that the bulk of humanity is slowly moving toward the next level of consciousness. This is actually far from the truth. A more accurate representation is that in recent history only those laggard souls who represent less than one-fifth of human souls have incarnated on the planet to make the next leap in consciousness, while the bulk of humanity who have already attained the higher levels have been sojourning on other planets in other dimensions and are ready to return to reclaim the planet. In fact, this process is already well under way.

World War II was a major turning point in the spiritual evolution of the Earth, because it was during this time frame that many laggard souls passed the third

initiation of consciousness and the planetary battle between the forces of light and dark was decisively won
by the forces of light. In the time frame of 1946, the
vast majority of advanced human souls made their decision to return to reclaim the planet and inaugurate a
new age. Not every soul who has come into incarnation
since 1947 is a part of this advance guard, nor would I
suggest that those who were born before the year 1946
are not as spiritual, but rather that large numbers of the
Baby Boom generation are. They are the spiritual
Green Berets. The counterforces that have ever sought
to keep the souls of humanity enslaved in ignorance
and fear were defeated in World War II, but they per-
sist in trying to maintain their hold over humanity,
seeking to confuse this incoming generation by dis-
tracting them from their true path to higher consciousness. This they do through counterfeit means, such as
mind-altering drugs, false gurus and bizarre cults, all of
which remotely resemble the true path, which includes
such practices as meditation, seeking the truth within
and possibly living within small democratic communal
groups focused on creating a better future for all.

As we enter the millennium, this point in time is
highly significant for a number of reasons, not least of
which is that as this advance guard of souls enters their
fifties collectively, they will begin to take an active part
on the world stage and organize themselves into
groups of all kinds to promote the spiritual welfare of
the planet. This will begin as their children, who have
consumed most of their time and energies, begin to
grow up and leave home.

Another reason that this time will be of significance
is that many will be entering their fifties, which is a time
of completion of seven times seven Earth years, and at

each seven-year cycle there is the possibility that a higher chakra will begin to exert an influence over the glandular system. The chakras are so named in Hindu philosophy because, seen with the inner vision, they appear as whirling wheels at intervals along the spine. The chakras are the seat of consciousness, and as consciousness rises, it moves up the spine to reside within a specific chakra that corresponds to a specific dimension.

Traditional teaching tells us that there are seven major chakras, but they should be conceptualized more as a continuum of 47 locations along the spine on the inner dimensions. Hence, for example, consciousness may begin at the lowest location, the base chakra at the base of the spine, and slowly move up seven locations.

Seen with the inner eye, the energy of the **first chakra**, or *base chakra*, may appear as a whirling red wheel that emits murky, blood-colored light energy. As consciousness rises, the color at the top of the chakra will be a clear rose-pink, signifying higher love, courage and enthusiasm. Because consciousness begins on the physical third dimension, it may initially be filled with lust, violent impulses and greed, but over time the nature will be refined to display higher qualities associated with physicality. The energy of the base chakra ties into the blood and the immune system.

The **second chakra** up from the base is related to the color orange and the fourth dimension, or astral plane. At a base level of consciousness this center emits dull orange energy, but as consciousness ascends, the light of a pure orange fills the individual energy field, which we call the aura. This second chakra is related to relationships, security and emotions, and it becomes active during puberty, stimulating growth and the sexual glands.

The **third chakra**, generally named the *solar plexus chakra*, is associated with the mental plane, the personal ego, the sense of personal identity and intelligent thinking. The energy coming through this center may begin as a dull mustard- yellow, and over lifetimes of increasing evolution fills the aura with clear yellow light. The chakra is related to the activity of neurotransmitters in the brain and is usually fully activated by age twenty-one.

For much of humanity, only the lower three chakras are activated, and the individual energy field is seen as a variety of red, orange and yellow hues, much like fire.

The **fourth chakra** is located at the level of the heart and is associated with the soul plane and the color green. When this chakra is activated and working at the highest level, a pure green healing energy is emitted through it.

The **fifth chakra** is located at the level of the throat and is associated with the buddhic plane, which is remote from the human personality. The energy coming through this center is related to both communication and telepathy and appears electric blue.

The **sixth chakra** is located at the level of the third eye and the pineal gland. It is related to inner vision and psychic ability, and deep indigo energy flows through it. This level is connected to the level of the monad, which is the individual divine spark that separated from All That Is.

The **crown chakra** at the top of the head is associated with transcendental unity, with All That Is on the atmic level. The energy coming through this center is violet, but when it is activated, the entire energy field becomes bright white, since violet completes the color spectrum and all the energies blend together to become white light energy.

At the completion of the seven-times-seven cycle, which will occur for many Baby Boomers during the beginning of the millennium, the higher chakras in the throat, third eye and crown will begin to activate for many who are spiritually inclined. These will produce neurotransmitters in the brain that will make a certain level of higher consciousness possible.

Many of the younger generation following the Baby Boomers have been referred to as the starseed generation — a group of human souls who have a higher consciousness and who have been together as a group on a more technologically advanced planet, awaiting the time of their return to Earth. This group has the capacity for telepathy, which is to say that many of them have attained the fifth-chakra level of consciousness in past lives and an attunement toward advanced technologies such as computers and the piloting of small craft. They are highly disoriented by their return to this planet, but at some future time they will begin to make major changes in the power and financial structures, since they find the existing system somewhat incomprehensible.

In addition to the waves of souls coming into incarnation to change the planet, there are vastly growing numbers of lightbeings coming to join the planet on the inner planes. They are here with interdimensional craft that anchor energies. These beings are a part of the greater Family of Light and come here from other planetary systems, similar to the chain of human evolution, to act as anchors for the influx of cosmic energies.

As the millennium marker has been approached and passed, many events are converging. The changes that will transform the planet have been carefully concerted since before your births. The transition to the new age will not happen overnight; it will be mainly brought about by wave after wave of advanced souls who will form a new humanity, while all individuals who are not under the influence of their higher selves will be slowly rerouted to a new planetary round.

As the vibrational speed of the planetary atoms approaches that of the fourth dimension, you will notice many changes, because the power of your thoughts and feelings will take on greater potency. That is because thoughts and feelings are actually tangible objects and energies in the higher dimensions, which is to say that they have an atomic structure and form on the fourth and fifth dimensions. These levels are causal to this reality and shape it. So as you draw closer to the fourth dimension, cause and effect become more instantaneous.

Much of what is initially required of you at this time is that you remember your spiritual identity — who you are and why you came here — and that you attempt to meditate daily as a point of entry for higher energies in the form of white light. Know that your higher self is not some remote, exalted being, but the *core* of you, the part of you that is creative, intelligent, humorous, altruistic, loving and knowing. As you engage in daily meditation to still the clamorous voices of your body, mind and emotions, your higher self will have the opportunity to make its voice heard and direct your thoughts, actions, intuitions and inspirations.

Another thought is this: Because of the recent developments, many of the older teachings you have studied that derive from older religions no longer apply to many of you, because you are not bound to incarnation by karma, and you have chosen to be here to inaugurate a change. Many of the difficult circumstances of your lives have not been your karma, but rather situations that you have created in order to develop certain traits. Also, there are many spiritual beings surrounding you with love who cannot interfere with your free will. This means that if you need help, you must request it. There is a vast array of beings who are stationed on the fifth dimension with the express purpose of responding to your needs.

2

Atlantis

I would like to spend some time discussing how the events of this present time in history tie in with the ancient civilization of Atlantis, a large continent that was situated in the Atlantic Ocean.

It is truly amazing to consider your current widely held beliefs about the development and evolution of humanity from primitive cavemen, when we here on the inner planes know and remember the truth of a culture so highly advanced that its like has never since been duplicated on Earth. Yet hints and traces of the truth exist for those who are willing to have open minds, for indeed the truth is too traumatic for the collective consciousness to face and accept. You have wiped from your minds the faintest remembrance and consciousness of Atlantis, for the terror and destruction was overwhelmingly devastating to you who were incarnate there at the time.

First, by thinking in terms of a civilization that was

ancient, you cannot find it in your imaginings, for the cities of Atlantis would be described by you as futuristic if you could see them in your mind's eye. They would look like your imaginings of Earth in the 23rd century.

Atlantis was a civilization that utilized an advanced technology and a science more evolved than you have today. They built spacious cities using energies and materials unheard of today. Also peculiar to Atlantis was their development of a variety of small airborne craft that were used much as automobiles are used today, inasmuch as every family had one or two. They also had oceangoing craft that traveled the seas rapidly and efficiently, but the citizenry preferred to be airborne.

You might be wondering why they did not escape the destruction that was to ensue. For the most part they did, but they were scattered around the Earth and lost most of their technology, which they had depended on.

To gain a clear appreciation of the civilization of Atlantis, it is necessary to understand the history of the world up to the inception of Atlantis. It was populated by a dark brown- to black-skinned people with curly hair and broad noses who came from the continent of Lemuria, which was in the Pacific and occupied some of what is now Antarctica. The forebears of the Atlanteans were also of this stock, but after a certain period on Atlantis, they mutated into a different racial type with straight hair, straight noses, narrow lips and skin that ranged from brown to light yellow. On Atlantis those from the north were fairer of hair and complexion than those to the south. Thus the world at the time of Atlantis was otherwise populated only by a dark-skinned people who were concentrated in Australia, India and Africa and who lived a simple lifestyle in small bands and villages without the organization of large cities.

The history of Atlantis spans a long period compared to modern civilizations. In the early stages it was still a fairly undeveloped culture; in the middle phase it was a highly advanced civilization both spiritually and scientifically; and at the end the emphasis was more on technology and science than on spirituality.

The story of Atlantis is long and complicated and far beyond the scope of a brief chapter such as this. The focus of this essay is to highlight the events in Atlantis pertinent to the spiritual awakening of the Age of Aquarius that is currently under way.

Atlantis existed in the cycle of involution — the descent into matter, which is the slowing of movement of electrons around their atomic nucleus, making matter more dense and somewhat harder to shape through the power of higher consciousness. The Atlanteans and their neighbors were initially more etheric than we are today, but gradually became more constrained by physical matter. That was the condition of the planet.

At present this planet has passed the nadir and is traveling back toward a higher vibrational mode that is more etheric. We are traveling away from the densest level of physical incarnation toward a more etheric, telepathic level of being. In the intervening time since the destruction of Atlantis, humanity has experienced a descent into the densest experience of incarnation possible and has been functioning without the inner contact to higher consciousness.

All this has been made more difficult because a group of high priest-scientists emerged from Atlantis, people who dedicated their beings to enslaving humanity in spiritual darkness and exploiting them for their own personal power — and we are still dealing with this situation today. This occurred because humanity has been given the gift of free will in order to broaden their experience, whereas other beings and kingdoms in nature have not, and they act always in accordance with divine will. I speak of the higher kingdoms of the angelic beings.

These dark brothers have always employed simple techniques as a means of gaining control of the lower chakras of humanity and inciting them to acts of evil and malice, which feeds into a vast pool of negative energy created by humanity on the third subplane of the lower astral plane. This astral matter, which is a tangible energy source on the inner planes, is composed of astral atoms generated by emotions such as anger, hatred, fear and guilt. It has become a collective evil with its own intelligence. This source of evil seeks to draw more of humanity into itself, recruiting new members and using these pawns to thwart the attempts of those who have a higher consciousness from doing good. The dark brothers are not in incarnation but have power from the astral plane over those whose consciousness is focused in the lower chakras and is primarily emotional in nature.

A number of theosophical teachers have told you that the dark brothers primarily work through those who have developed the lower psychism, but this is not actually true. The focus of control is not through the lower psychism, but through having a consciousness focused on the three lower chakras and being responsive to negative emotions.

We are at the end of a 2000-year cycle. It was promised that Jesus died for the sins of humanity and has taken away human sin. He is to return and descend to the third subplane of the astral plane and dispel the collective energy of evil that has accumulated there because there is no other way to deal with it. Only a Christ with an army of christed beings can dispel such an energy accumulation. This has yet to occur. (I interchange the names of the masters Jesus Sananda and Christ because the Master Jesus was overlit by the consciousness of the Master Maitreya in the office of Christ.) You may imagine that this is an event to be anticipated and desired with great celebration, and the gathering on the inner planes of many masters and spiritual beings who have experienced other planets is the gathering together of an army of beings who are not only working to accelerate the natural evolutionary arc of this beautiful turquoise planet, but who will themselves also descend from the higher mental planes to the lower astral planes.

The scenario played out in Atlantis that culminated in the destruction of the continent inaugurated an era lasting for perhaps 10,000 years, during which time forces of materialism and ignorance held sway. This long period of darkness and horror has continued because this planetary school is a freewill planet. It is something of a cosmic alternative school where the souls here devise their own curriculum. The time has come to close this school as it is currently functioning and redirect those forces that have been in effect here since the time of Atlantis, redesigning this planetary school.

To shift direction and return to the effects of the destruction of Atlantis, the Old Testament of the Bible is an interesting document for a number of reasons. It is very old, and it is a collection of stories that abounded in the Middle East in Sumerian, Chaldean and Egyptian mythology. The first six chapters were compiled by Moses, an Egyptian prince who had access to the libraries of documents written in hieroglyphs that detailed the stories of other ancient cultures. Moses described the Great Flood, which relates to Atlantis and was in the historic writings of many peoples of the Middle East, including the Egyptians and Sumerians. Unfortunately, the description of the Great Flood paints an inaccurate picture because it was written long after the actual event. It is inaccurate also because it states that only Noah and his family survived it, which was not the case. Many people survived and were scattered in isolated groups. However, the most interesting aspect of the story of Moses is that the Egyptian culture was a remnant of the Atlantean, and Moses had access to Atlantean devices and beliefs.

Also of interest are the even more ancient Indian texts written in Sanskrit. Many of these documents refer to small groups of people who escaped from Atlantis at the time of its destruction.

At the time of the destruction of Atlantis, there were some large colonies on other continents, principally in China and South America. However, most of those who escaped by aircraft flew to India, Tibet, Egypt, Chaldea, Sumer and parts of North America and even more obscure places, such as small islands.

The Atlanteans were a devastated people because they found themselves isolated in small groups and without the technologies they depended on. So inevitably, they intermarried with the black-skinned populations and began re-creating cities with temples such as they were accustomed to.

A large contingent moved to India, and over time

moved in small groups into Europe. Those who moved to Europe were, for the most part, northern Atlanteans, and those who had previously colonized the Orient were southern Atlanteans. Both groups mutated somewhat in their new conditions, basically because of limited gene pools. Those in the Middle East were a mixture of Atlanteans with a dash of indigenous black peoples.

Confusing as this seems, the history of the movements and mixtures of the peoples of Earth is even more so. Many historical accounts that people wonder about today, thinking they might be in reference to aliens, actually refer to Atlanteans. Some of the weapons and flying vehicles were maintained by small colonies for hundreds of years, but eventually the means of repairing and maintaining such vehicles was forgotten. So it was that Atlanteans could appear out of the sky to a distant group of people and be venerated as gods and described as angels. The most technologically and spiritually advanced colony was probably the one in Egypt, but the most spiritually *wise* colony was in Tibet.

During the heyday of Atlantis before the destruction, a divine incarnation named Melchizedek created the Atlantean temple system, which was aligned with the seven cosmic rays. There were seven orders, although there were more than seven temples. There were temples of science and technology, political science, arts and music and dance. There were also temples of education, psychic development and seership and one of ritual magic. The minority of Atlanteans in the order lived a disciplined lifestyle that included daily yoga, meditation, study and so on. The average Atlantean followed an exoteric religion that was similar to Chinese Taoism.

When the Atlanteans were split and scattered, they did not have a uniform belief system. Those from specific temples went to specific places. The existing colonies were somewhat inhospitable, since they had dissented and split from Atlantis, and few Atlanteans relished the idea of going to China or South America. So one large contingent settled in the Mesopotamian basin and another formed the higher castes of India. These were north Atlantean peoples, some of whom journeyed into Europe in successive waves and became known as Celtic, Germanic and Hellenic peoples. Genetically speaking, the descendants of the Atlanteans are everywhere, composing all racial types except black, who are of Lemurian descent, as were the Atlanteans.

My point is that originally there was one unified set of mystery teachings that existed in the temples of Atlantis. After the continent sank, the teachings were fragmented around the planet. The ancient Egyptians had a story about the god Osiris and his consort Isis, in which Osiris was killed and cut into pieces, which Isis searched the Earth for so that she could put him back together. This is a nice metaphor for the mystery teachings. Helena Blavatsky could be likened to Isis. She studied the religions from many sources, and with her peers she pieced them together to form the teachings of the Theosophical Society, influencing many other esoteric groups.

This information is relevant because we are rapidly approaching a time when science has uncovered some of the same technologies that led to the downfall and destruction of Atlantis. It is also relevant that many of the souls who attained the highest levels of development in the Atlantean temple system, who graduated from the Earth school of the White Brotherhood and moved on to other planetary rounds, have elected to return at this time. The central problem of Atlantis was that science and technology became separated from spirituality, and scientists began to violate some of the spiritual principles and ethics that had existed at an earlier time.

One of their main interests was their attempt to create an improved human type by playing around with genetics. Their goal was to create a strain of human with a stronger immune system and more resistance to disease and ultraviolet rays. For the most part, nothing of any lasting significance came of these experiments. There were also experiments with nuclear weaponry and controlling the weather, and while playing around with these powerful forces, the Atlanteans unleashed forces that destroyed their continent and scattered the survivors in small groups all over the globe.

The scenario we are moving into is this: The forces that led to the destruction of Atlantis are at play in the world today, but a vast number of souls who moved through the Atlantis experience have come back to prevent a second occurrence of this catastrophe and cooperate in accelerating the planet to higher frequency levels.

Of special interest to observe, as this drama unfolds on the world stage, is that at the time of the fall of Atlantis there was a political leader who was a high initiate of the priestly order, a man of vision and wisdom, who opposed the direction in which the scientist-priests were going. His opponents started a campaign of lies and humiliation that swayed the masses against him and led to the eventual destruction of the continent. He has returned today to resume his leadership role, and the forces that were long ago arrayed against him have continued their tactics of humiliation. What is interesting is that the mass of souls incarnated at this time have unconscious memories of the consequences of turning against this man, so now they have refused to be swayed by attacks aimed at his personal frailties. How these dramas play out on the world stage will affect the outcome of planetary events.

3

The Seven Rays

To begin this discussion I would like you to use your imagination to picture the vast emptiness of space before creation as empty darkness stretched infinitely in every direction. Then try to imagine the very opposite: Partitioned off from space, imagine a vast sea of light and consciousness stretching in every direction. Try to imagine within the light all the forms of creation as ephemeral images, appearing and disappearing, being potentially dreamed of in the consciousness of the Creator. Everything in the light is in equilibrium, at rest, and there is only one consciousness, the consciousness of All That Is, which contains within Itself the potential for everything that will ever be created.

Now imagine a small rent in the fabric of space, in the partition between All That Is and All That is Not. We will refer to this rent as the Source. Through this rent in space, Source breathes emanations out into the vastness of space. We shall think of the first emanation as a feminine principle, which takes the form of billions of protons projected into space. Needless to say, I am simplifying something more complicated and skirting the issue of neutrons.

The vastness of space fills with a limitless sea of protons. By their nature they are very small, but they exist nevertheless, and they have mass and weight. Thus what we have here is hydrogen ions, but actually smaller and lighter. Eventually, by their own innate tendency to rest, they fill space and stop moving. They are magnetically drawn to each other and begin to form groups of protons that orbit each other, linked in a magnetic bond. They also begin to arrange themselves by weight, as nearer or farther from Source, forming throughout space octaves based on weight. The heavier groups fall farther away from Source. (At this point, this is a metaphor rather than a scientific reality, so do not become confused.)

The second emanation from Source is light. We might think of this as a masculine principle and as electrons that have boundless energy and never rest. These electrons emanated from Source through the vastness of space, traveling at high speeds, and they were eventually captured by the magnetic attraction exerted by the protons. So instead of traveling linearly away from Source, they traveled in orbits around the protons.

This process is the divine marriage between the feminine and masculine principles and results in all the various dimensions of existence, of which there are seven, each with seven subdivisions. Atoms closer to the Source are lighter in atomic weight and have electrons whirling around them. They travel at much faster speeds than atoms manifested on the physical plane.

These electrons moving around the atomic nucleus at speeds faster than the speed of light are beyond our perception, and the orbits are different because the density and mass of the nuclei are different from those of the third dimension. To summarize, the protons of the higher dimension have less density and mass and the electrons move faster and have wider orbits.

Does this description of the creation have a familiar ring? "There was stillness over the face of the deep, and the Lord said, "Let there be light." Also, the oriental symbol of yin and yang seems to be contained in this imagery. I am suggesting that there was a time when this understanding of atoms was known by the wise and that they described the process of creation within their terminology. Out of the Middle East tradition comes the imagery of water and light, and out of the oriental tradition comes the imagery of light and dark. In the Hindu tradition we have reference to the outbreaths of Brahma.

In the beginning, all the atoms arranged themselves into octaves of frequencies, which created the seven major dimensions of reality, with the lightest, highest-frequency atoms close to Source and the densest being farthest away. Also, a limit was placed in the emptiness of space so that no atom could travel so far from the Source that it could never return.

Within these seven major octaves are seven subdimensions. Perhaps in your minds you begin to see this taking the image of concentric rings, which is a good image as far as it goes, but all these dimensions occupy the same space and interpenetrate each other. The atoms also arranged themselves in chains down through the dimensions, which are somewhat like an onion — spherical, with many layers.

We might imagine that when the structure of the universe had taken shape, the Mother principle filled the void and the Father principle joined with her to create the raw stuff. Then the third principle emanated from Source, which was the Son, and this emanation took the form of sparks, which did not fill all the created universe, but only that dimension closest to Source. These sparks became the Stella Logoi, which are the consciousnesses of the stars. Around these sparks, ninth-dimension atoms coalesced. Over time, some but not all of these stars descended through the dimensions, always having a core of atoms from the higher dimensions. Realize, however, that not all the stars sank to the lowest level. Know that these stellar beings have a divine consciousness and that they are beings.

Each star being is a cocreator with All That Is and creates its own solar system, planets and the forms of the lives on them. Various successive emanations from Source created the angelic realms, the human sparks and other cosmic beings.

I began this topic with the seven rays. At this point there have been emanations from Source, but these are not the seven rays. When all of the consciousnesses were in place, Source emitted a continuous flow of energy as white light, which on the ninth dimension splits into seven rays. These energies flow down through all the planes and subplanes, and different agents act as transformers for them.

In the esoteric books these rays are named as the rays of Will, Love/Wisdom, Intelligent Activity, Healing and Arts, Harmony through Conflict, Devotion and Ceremonial Magic. A quick mental analysis will reveal that these are apples and oranges and that these words do not convey energies that are in the same class. Thus we are mentally on safe ground when we describe energy in terms of light and heat, but on shaky ground when we try to think of energies as something else.

As thinkers, you try to separate energy from its source. The Sun is by nature hot and light, so its energy is heat and light. The atoms of your body interplay with the emanations from the Sun, so when you are exposed to sunlight, you receive heat and light. In similar fashion, the seven rays emanate from the Source and share Its attributes.

References to the rays in the past have emphasized their effect on the level of the higher selves, which is related to purpose in incarnation. In other words, if a soul is incarnating on a particular ray, it is coming in to work in a particular field such as leadership and law, science, education, religion, healing and so on. This is puzzling if one is a store clerk or a salesperson, because the seven rays do not cover all fields of endeavor.

So in general it might be easier to conceptualize the cosmic rays as colors and realize that they change in nature according to the dimension they are moving through. For example, let's take the ray of Will (which I find an unfortunate term because it conjures up concepts such as willpower, a mental straining to control oneself, or the imposition of one's will upon another) and assign to it a correspondence to the color red. Now conceptualize it as a ray of *intent* on the soul level. Other correspondences are training in the military, politics or law on the mental level, courage and enthusiasm on the emotional level and self-discipline on the physical level. This gives us a better sense of how the rays function in different dimensions.

A ray is a constant energy force that has different effects and implications as it moves though the different dimensions or planes. On the plane of soul, the sixth dimension, the field of the higher self, the rays are related to an expression of a particular purpose for a particular length of time. The purpose is related to becoming really good in some particular field of endeavor, much as choosing a major in a university program. However, the nature of the rays changes in their application as they move through other dimensions.

What this amounts to is that each one of you reading this, every human soul, is on one of the rays, so it is as if you are part of a vast team. Each ray has one or more masters anchoring the energy of the ray on this planet in the fifth dimension. The energy comes down from the sixth dimension and continues on to the fourth and third dimensions. The masters are the central points of the inner-plane ashrams, and the energy enters the planet through them. (An inner-plane ashram is a group of souls clustered around a master or group of masters.) All souls on the spiritual path are arranged around the masters in the ashram from nearby to farther away, according to the level of the energy of the ray they can transmit. The ascension process is a process of disciplines and exercises designed to raise the ability of the individual to transmit and transform the energy of a specific ray, thereby moving closer toward the heart of the ashram, toward the master. This, of course, is not accomplished by attending a few workshops and group meditations, but is the culmination of many lifetimes of effort.

It is necessary to understand that the seven rays are entering the planet and are moving through all of you through your chakra systems. As you attain purity in the highest levels of consciousness — physically, emotionally, mentally and spiritually — these rays flow through the lower four chakras. At this point, the higher self has control over the personality.

The temples of the masters exist in the fifth dimension as solid structures constructed on the chakras of the planetary being, which are entry points for the seven cosmic rays into the planetary system. They take the form of buildings, temples of great beauty. The temples of fabled Atlantis were the physical manifestation of these inner temples.

The first ray, that of intent, which I will conceptualize as the red ray, emanates through the Temple of Will, which is the gathering point for the ashram of the Master Morya. Those whose souls are on this ray are working through law and legislation and with themes of leadership roles and patterns for civilizations, such as politicians, corporate and military leaders, architects and city planners.

The second ray of Love/Wisdom, which expresses through the color orange-gold, is the ashram of the Master Kuthumi, and I am associated with this ashram. Those whose primary focus or soul intent is on this ray are involved in dispensing the wisdom teachings through religious groups, mystery schools and other teachings. They are also involved in counseling skills and psychology. In the distant past, astrology was used as a tool to help the individual find the purpose of his or her incarnation.

The third ray, the yellow ray, is that of intellect and Intelligent Activity and is the ashram of Paul the Venetian. Those who are on this ray are focused on education and research, such as university professors. This ray also pertains to all activist groups.

The fourth ray, corresponding to the color green, is the ashram of Serapis Bey and ties in to the healing sciences, art and beauty.

The fifth ray, the blue ray, is focused through the Temple of Harmony through Conflict, the ashram of Hilarion. This is the ray of communications, science, mathematics and music, which might be thought of as the ray of geometric correspondences and harmonics.

The indigo ray is that of seership and mysticism, devotion and idealism and comprises the Temple of Devotion of Sananda.

The seventh ray of Ceremonial Magic, the violet ray, is focused through the ashram of St. Germain. This ray is a synthesis of attributes of the other rays and a higher level of the first ray. Themes of this ray are associated with consciously invoking higher forces to work with form.

What I am stating here that might be considered new or different is that I would prefer that esoteric students conceive of the seven rays as a rainbow of energies streaming continuously through the dimensions, energizing the life forms on these different levels. These rays are not actually colored, but we might think of them as having a specific color in order to make correspondences easier.

Of course, these seven ray correspondences to masters are not set in stone, and different masters come in and out of these ashrams and anchor various energies. At this time each ashram has various additional masters who are not generally well-known.

It is possible to visit these temples in meditation by the use of intent. Many have heard of the violet flame of St. Germain, which may be used to transmute negative energy patterns, but all the masters and temples have a flame that may be used to purify one's consciousness in one way or another. The white light is the synthesis of all the rays and is the ray of the Christ. It is the white light that is used to protect and to connect spiritually to the higher powers.

Some are familiar with the pathworkings of the kabbalistic system, which uses spheres on the astral plane that are ruled by various powerful devic, elemental and angelic forces. You may read of a specific sphere that is ruled by a particular God-force, and you may go there in meditation and learn something of the nature of this location. These kabbalistic spheres exist at a lower level than the temples and ashrams of the masters, but they correspond to them. The temples are in the fifth dimension and the kabbalistic spheres in the fourth dimension. Also, the seven major archangels from Judaic tradition correspond to the rays, and their different activities correspond to properties of the rays, such as protection, healing, communication, arts and beauty, harmony and so on.

While the focus of the temples and ashrams in the fifth dimension is on specific streams of activity, much like a large university might have many different departments that offer many majors as fields of study, the kabbalistic spheres relate to the development of traits of character, since they are part of the fourth dimension or the astral plane, which is a realm of emotions and feelings. As the student travels through the spheres described in the Tree of Life work by creative meditation, he or she works on acquiring the traits that pertain to the spheres. On this level the seven rays manifest themselves as attributes of character such as courage and enthusiasm, wisdom and compassion, intelligence, joy and devotion.

On the physical level, the individual is under the influence of a soul ray and a personality ray. The interplay of these two forces, one being one's life's purpose and the other being one's most typical form of self-expression, results in infinite combinations of personality types and personal expression.

4

The Etheric Levels

You know that the physical plane is described as being composed of solids, liquids and gas, or sometimes in terms of the elements as Earth, air, fire and water. But in esoteric writings there is frequent reference to something called ether, which is described as being a more refined level of the physical dimension. In this discussion I would like to focus a little on the nature of the etheric realm.

The gases you are familiar with on your planet are composed of fairly simple atoms that do not attach to each other. The simplest atomic structure in your physical reality is the hydrogen ion, which is a positively charged nucleus of an atom, or a single proton. The hydrogen atom is only slightly more complicated in that it is composed of a positively charged nucleus and a negatively charged electron. What then, would be finer, more ethereal, less tangible than a simple gas, yet still be defined as existing at the higher levels of physical reality? The answer must surely and clearly be those electrons that are not bound to a nucleus and travel rapidly through space as particles of light and radiation, depending on their speed and wavelength.

What you consider to be empty space or a vacuum is filled with particles traveling at tremendously high speeds in every direction. There are particles emitted by the physical Sun and particles that were emitted perhaps millions of years ago by distant stars that have finally reached this area of space. These particles are infinitely small and not visible in space. They become measurable or tangible only when they enter the atmosphere of the Earth.

Perhaps you know that light particles travel in group waves and form various wavelengths. There are short and long wavelengths, and the wavelengths of particles interact with the nerve endings in the retinas of your eyes to form colors. There may be colors that exist beyond your eyesight's ability to recognize them, just as people with color blindness cannot perceive certain colors. So beyond the scope of human eyesight, there are other forms of light such as x-rays and ultraviolet radiation, all created by particles moving in waves.

All that you know and have learned about heat and light you know from your observations of sunlight, as well as scientific experiments on a variety of substances to create heat and light sources electronically or with atomic and nuclear reactions. If other types of stars transmitted other types of radiation, you would not know anything about them because they are too distant. All you know about radiation is based on the Sun.

So the Sun is by nature a heat, light and radiation transmitter, continuously pulsing particles outward in a variety of different wave formations. The Sun is also capable of pulsing particles outward at speeds faster than the speed of light. These form the higher ethers and are undetectable by you. Naturally, these high-speed particles also come in a variety of short and long wave patterns.

If there were no Sun, of course, there would be no life on Earth. This lovely planet, which teems with a myriad of life forms, would be a frozen rock in space. Also, the planet is just exactly the right mass, in the right orbit and at the right speed for the planet to be neither too hot nor too cold for life. When you think about it, this is a most amazing fact. But from the viewpoint of the ancient wisdom teachings, the Sun is an intelligent and ensouled being referred to as the Solar Logos, and the Earth is an intelligent and ensouled being referred to by many names such as Terra or Gaia, and on a higher level as the Planetary Logos. The light, heat and radiation emanating from the Sun to the Earth is a manifestation of the love and wisdom of the Solar Logos for Terra, which makes life forms possible. The Solar Logos also permeates this part of space with ethers, which are high-speed, high-frequency particles. Of course, there is no part of space that does not have ethers, because these particles are being transmitted by billions of Solar Logoi in all directions.

In the 1940s physicists were astonished to learn that a single particle can be influenced by the expectations of an observer, and this little discovery turned science topsy-turvy, making nonsense of every theory ever set forth. In general they do not broadcast this information and the general public is not familiar with it, but nevertheless it is true: *Thought affects subatomic particles.* Take a moment to think about this scientific fact: *The expectations of an observer affect the behavior of sub-*

atomic particles. Thus thought shapes the ethers.

I would like to make it clear here that there are levels of matter and energy all around you that interpenetrate your reality. You are unaware of them because they are beyond the abilities of your five senses to register, but this does not make them any less real. There are naturally seven major wavelengths of ethers — and there are also higher and finer forms of electricity, magnetism, radiation and light. These are the raw material of manifestation, because when any particle becomes trapped in the orbit of a proton, it becomes part of an atom, and becomes neutral.

So there are a number of comments that need to be made about the etheric level, which is a higher and finer level of physical manifestation. First, there are beings whose point of incarnation stops at the ethers. They move and have their being all around you, yet you are not aware of their presence. The second point of interest is that all forms of creation must have an etheric counterpart for there to be a form in the first place. The third point is that it is through Earth's *etheric body* that its energy is being accelerated toward the fourth dimension.

You might be wondering how all these rapidly moving particles, which are not bound to an atomic nucleus, could bind together to hold a form and not go whizzing off into space. They are bound by the power of thought. You might begin to notice when you meditate or when you imagine yourself filled with white light that you are using concentrated, focused thought, which is very powerful, to create your etheric lightbody, and that when you send out light to the planet and hold the planet in light and love, you affect the etheric body of the planet. This is why we have called you lightworkers. You are working with light, and lightbeings are all around you working with you.

I am now revealing a deep mystery: *Love speeds up the movement of electrons*. I have already stated that an observer's thoughts affect the direction of movement of an electron — and this is a demonstrated scientific fact — so it should not be too difficult to imagine that the energy of love, or loving thoughts, makes electrons (which form the ethers and orbit the nuclei of atoms) travel faster. This is what spiritually aware people mean when they talk about "raising the vibration."

The greatest daily act of service to the planet and yourself is to take time at the beginning or end of each day and imagine yourself being completely hollow. Visualize yourself filling up with clear, bright, pure white light and linking with other lightworkers and organizations, holding them in the light and seeing the entire planet enfolded in light. When you do this, you become an anchor for a chain of beings who exist on the etheric, the astral and the mental levels. This work of anchoring the light is more important than channeling wisdom teachings, although it may be less glamorous.

The more time and effort you lightworkers spend visualizing and holding the light, the brighter and stronger your light will be. Have confidence that it is there and is visible to etheric beings. Also remember that the reason you came into incarnation, among other things, was to raise your level of light. Many of you imagine that you have come into incarnation in order to create your own reality as a priority, and you expect to manifest money, relationships and the things your heart desires. You find to your disappointment that this does not occur. This is because your highest good and greatest light may involve what you might consider deprivation and hardship in order to learn the lessons that will make you a brighter light.

On the other hand, I would tell you that you are creating your own reality and that it is time to stop believing that poverty or sexual abstinence or suffering are a required part of the spiritual path. If you believe these things are part of the path, that is surely what you will draw to yourself. You must understand that your soul is engineering your reality in order to force you to increase your light. Remember too that the majority of you who are reading this have undertaken to incarnate as a large team of lightworkers and that you are following a divine plan that was conceptualized before your birth.

There are many aspects to this divine plan that you have contracted to be a part of, so although you might imagine that you are following personal goals and trying to establish your place in the world in regard to work and family, you are also doing your piece in helping this plan to unfold. Many aspects of the plan are unfolding simultaneously. There are at this time a number of etheric energy vortices around the planet, which comprise the etheric chakras of the planetary being. Since these sacred sites are part of a planetary chakra system, they are anchoring points for different kinds of energy and correspond to the seven cosmic rays. Each of you has a higher self that is on a specific ray, and each ray has a special significance. Thus people are being drawn to congregate in groups at these sacred sites around the planet in order to anchor the energies of that particular ray. The most important work to be performed at these sites is the anchoring of its energy by groups of meditating lightworkers. This is the beginning of the work of externalizing the ashrams of the masters.

Also of interest at this time is that the ranks of those souls in the inner-plane ashrams are swelling as souls from other star systems arrive to assist in the process of accelerating the evolution of this planet. They come with great joy and eagerness to serve in what is a uniquely rare opportunity to display compassion and usefulness in the process of putting an end to the general misery and suffering that has been the common experience of souls incarnate on Earth.

5

Toward a Cosmic Psychology of Being

I would like to discuss an ambitious topic, so I'll offer a short preface to explain that this is an ambitious undertaking. I am working by projecting a stream of thought into the mind of the receiver, much like sending out a radio transmission. The thoughts are received and dressed up in the receiver's own words, and it is possible in this process for a thought to be missed or slightly changed because the mind of the receiver may contain certain biases that warp the incoming stream of thought. In this essay I will attempt to discuss, somewhat like a juggling performance, the effects of the ongoing shift from the third to the fourth dimension in terms of the effects it will have on the personal and collective unconscious minds of those incarnate on this planet.

Your third-dimensional reality consists of atoms,

which have electrons whirling around them at a specific speed. Because the limit in your dimension is the speed of light, when anything goes faster than that it becomes invisible. The higher dimensions are composed of atoms whose electrons move incrementally faster than those of your dimension, faster than the speed of light.

It would be easier to understand what I am saying if I started from Source and suggested that all atoms originally issued from Source at very high speeds, and as they traveled farther and farther away, they naturally arranged themselves in octaves. Those farthest from Source formed the slowest and densest levels of matter. Of course, all these levels of matter interpenetrate, so there is no near or far in actuality. It is somewhat analogous to a cooling-off process, just as water vapor condenses into water droplets when cooled and into snowflakes at even cooler temperatures. Your third-dimension reality is the coolest and densest level of reality, metaphorically speaking. Beyond it are other dimensions that follow different laws of physics and where particles and electrons move at a faster rate.

As the electrons of your planetary atoms accelerate toward the frequency of the fourth dimension, it would be helpful to understand some of the changes this process will bring. It will help to understand something about the fourth dimension, which I call the astral plane, and the fifth dimension, which I call the mental plane.

What I am attempting to do would not be possible if your brains were not in the nature of receivers and transmitters that receive thoughts from your mental body (located on the mental plane) and emotions from your emotional body (located on the astral plane).

Since all matter on one level has a matrix on the next higher level, the astral plane is composed of thoughts that are charged with feelings. The mental body is composed of the atoms of the mental plane, which is in turn composed of an octave of frequencies. The mental body is a replica of the physical body in an ovoid of mental-plane atoms attached to your physical body.

Thoughts on the mental plane are tangible objects composed of atoms of the mental plane. Thoughts are formed by thought waves, which crystallize the matter of the mental-plane atmosphere into small, dense objects. They take the form of tiny pictures, recognizable objects or geometrical shapes suspended in the mental body. Some of them rotate or orbit, whereas others remain still or slowly fade away. If they are set in motion, their vibrations through the "air" of the mental plane set up thought waves, which are transmitted through the mental plane.

A strong, clear thought with emotion attached to it will precipitate into the astral plane and become clothed in astral matter. A matrix continues to exist on the mental plane, but on the astral plane the thought will become energetic and dynamic. Objects on the astral plane are composed of atoms whose electrons move faster than the speed of light. Therefore they are luminous, starry or astral in appearance. One might imagine thought forms that have precipitated onto the astral plane as something similar to tiny Christmas tree ornaments, hanging in the air, glittering, twinkling, rotating and chiming. However, they are extremely tiny and are very potent in relation to their size. Some of them are as ephemeral as soap bubbles in sunlight.

So you see that we are beginning to touch on a vast topic with many possible ramifications. High above the highest known sound frequencies are the feeling and emotional frequencies and thought frequencies that can be received and transmitted though the human brain. What I wish to stress here is that the personality of an individual goes far beyond the limits of the human brain and exists at tremendously high frequencies of matter, which we call higher dimensions. Not only are there bodies on these higher planes that are attached to the physical body, but emotionally charged thoughts generated by the personality are suspended in the energy field or orbit the body or sometimes even project outward toward someone else.

Most individuals do not have only one counterpart on the astral plane, but a small *group* of astral selves that have separated from the personality through the process of growing up and developing a personal identity. This is a very important concept to grasp, because many books describe the astral body as being only one counterpart to the physical body, an exact duplicate. This exact duplicate is the conscious personality, the personality being threefold in nature and consisting of physical, emotional and mental elements. On the astral level, many selves split off from the conscious self and form unconscious selves. This process of dealing with and integrating the many unconscious astral selves is the basis of most forms of psychotherapy.

At this point it might be pertinent to direct the discussion to the work of the founders of psychology at the end of the last century and the beginning of this century, who attempted to chart a topography of the psyche, thought to be within the brain. Sigmund Freud divided the personality into the id, which is roughly the astral self, and the ego, which is the conscious mental self. The higher self more truly corresponds to Jung's concept of the Self. Freud also divided consciousness into a conscious and an unconscious level, and Carl Jung added the concept of the collective unconscious, which is filled with archetypal images and racial memories. From the point of view of these men, these concepts represented subjective consciousness based somewhere in the brain.

I am suggesting that these concepts represent objective realities that follow laws different from those of the physical plane, realities that are located on these higher dimensions. The total personality takes the form of a house on the astral plane. Well-lit areas of the house represent the conscious mind and a dark cellar represents the unconscious. Lurking in the dark of the cellar is the unconscious self, a monster or evil twin who represents all the traits that the individual personality has disowned, refused to love or refused to accept. This being has been referred to in occult literature as the Dweller on the Threshold (although I prefer "the Dweller in the Cellar") and as the shadow by Carl Jung. I might add that Jung was influenced by ancient Gnostic texts, which were in turn influenced by Zoroastrian thought. So the general concept of the shadow self is not entirely modern. Also lurking in this house is the anima or animus, an opposite gender entity that is a repository of all unconscious thoughts and feelings about members of the opposite sex. The anima or animus could be a negative or a positive entity, or there might be one of each.

The astral plane, or fourth dimension, toward which the planet is rapidly accelerating in atomic frequency, contains physical locations composed of high- frequency matter where each individual in incarnation has an astral home peopled with dissociated parts of his or her personality. These aspects of the self and thoughts and emotions that take on a human form are in the darkness, not in the light of consciousness. They are more powerful in their effects than those thoughts and selves that are conscious and in the light. They play havoc with the life of the individual and may do so in a number of ways. On one level these unconscious dissociated selves serve to attract people and circumstances that match their vibrations, so individuals may find themselves surrounded by people who mirror their unconscious negative traits and who are in conflict with them. Or they may find themselves in relationships filled with repeating patterns of conflict.

Another means by which these unconscious thoughts, feelings and traits, which take the form of human personalities, play havoc with the individual are in moments of unconsciousness when they take over the personality and behave and talk in ways that conflict with the ideals of the conscious self. A typical example of this might be when an individual has had a few drinks and becomes increasingly uninhibited, displaying uncharacteristic humor, emotion, sexuality or violence. The unconscious self leaps into the driver's seat and replaces the conscious self, who is serious, unemotional, sexually repressed and nonviolent. The change is so out of character that when the individual is told all that he or she said and did under the influence of alcohol, he finds it hard to believe.

The interesting part about locating these conscious and unconscious elements of the personality in another dimension, as opposed to somewhere in the brain, is that it is possible for there to be communication with individuals on the astral plane of which the individual is not aware or which may emerge in dreams. This is the basis for the idea of the collective unconscious, a level where all humanity can communicate with each other and synchronous events can be planned. Added to the complexity of all this, many beings have their existence on the astral level or fourth dimension. This makes it similar to the descriptions of events in *Alice in Wonderland* and *Through the Looking Glass.*

Defense mechanisms are a final group of thoughts within the conscious self on the astral plane. These have been constructed by the self to defend itself from having to face anxiety-provoking truths. When the individual constructs too many defense mechanisms, the self becomes totally out of touch with reality and the unconscious astral self completely sweeps away the ego structure, flooding the consciousness with unconscious content. This is called psychosis. Defense mechanisms can be viewed as a wall or barrier of thoughts. They include rationalization, justification, projection, intellectualization, reaction formation, hysterical conversion and outright denial that there is a problem.

An important task, therefore, as we enter this period of slow ascension toward the fourth dimension, is for each individual to do the necessary work to integrate the many selves on the astral level, illuminate the unconscious thought forms and dismantle and remove the defense mechanisms. As the frequencies of the planet increase, the effects of the astral plane on the physical plane will increase, and many people will experience this as an increase in the level of interpersonal conflict and uncomfortable circumstances in their lives.

Now I propose to briefly discuss some simple methods currently in use in therapies and spiritual books. They include positive affirmations, visualizations,

meditations, dream analysis — and the most important
of all, which involves integrating the unconscious
selves into the conscious self by forgiveness, accep-
tance, recognition and love. First, simply write on a
piece of paper those qualities in others that annoy you
the most. However, realize that these traits are in you
as well and while you may be unaware of them, your
friends and family are not. If you hate cruelty, your
family might view you as cruel; if you hate judgmental
people, your family might view you as judgmental and
so on. They have witnessed those moments when your
unconscious evil twin took over your personality.

There is a method used in Psychosynthesis that requires the individual to visualize a house, then enter it
and meet the beings there. This is a very helpful visual-
ization, especially if the individual goes down into the
cellar, turns on a light and looks to see who and what
are down there. By bringing the subpersonalities into a
lighted room and talking to them, they cease to be unconscious; they are welcomed into the light of consciousness.

This, my dear ones, is truly important spiritual
work. Another important piece of this process is to
take time to consciously forgive everyone from your
past whom you have not forgiven and release them
with love. You do this, not for their benefit, but to release yourself from the bondage of unforgiveness.
Learn to live your life without hating or resisting anything, for you give whatever you hate and resist power
over you in your unconscious mind located in the
fourth dimension.

Take the time to find the areas of your life where re-
peated negative patterns emerge, whether in the work-
place or in relationships, and deduce from that what

kind of negative thought might be creating these experiences, even if you have no recollection of ever holding such a thought. It is unconscious, so you cannot know that you have this thought in your energy field. This is where many books on this subject are confusing; they imply that you are consciously holding a negative thought. So mentally affirm the opposite and realize that visualizations are a means of consciously entering the astral plane and making changes there that will effectively change your life.

I hope you are beginning to see that taking the time and effort to do this is not time and energy wasted. You are effecting changes in other realities, and these other realities are causal to your reality.

6

Inhabitants of the Fourth Dimension

In this discussion I wish to present information by using models, paradigms and constructs, and I would not wish the reader to mistake any of these ideas as absolute truths. I have attempted to stretch the mind of the reader to imagine that reality might seem to be a certain way but that at a later time, in order to grow, it may be necessary for you to cast aside some of these constructs as simply exercises in a certain way of thinking.

Technology has advanced so greatly during this century that it is possible to use many technological advances as analogies. Thus if I were to state that life is somewhat analogous to a virtual reality game, many of you would understand this concept, which would not be possible if technology were not so advanced. Those of us who teach may use paradigms and constructs and refer to the current technology in order to illustrate a point.

Now I would like to continue the theme of how the gradually rising atomic frequency of this planet will draw everything closer to the fourth dimension or astral plane and how this will affect everyday lives in the near future.

At this point I wish to make a leap and give some descriptions of the nature of the fourth dimension. The most important aspect of the fourth dimension is that it is the home, or focus of consciousness, of the angelic, elemental and devic kingdom. This is one vast group of beings who are known in the Hindu tradition as devas and in the Christian tradition as angels, though these words have slightly different connotations. However, we are essentially talking about the same kingdom of beings. These beings can be viewed as vortexes of whirling colored energy, so I would like you to hold the image in your mind of great and small vortexes of whirling light and color. Through hundreds of thousands of years of association with the human kingdom, all these energy beings have assumed the appearance of some kind of solid human form in the fourth dimension, but their true nature is pure energy.

I have mentioned before that every object in the third dimension has an energy matrix in the fourth dimension that serves to hold it together. The angelic and devic kingdom works with the energy matrices of forms in the fourth dimension, so they are caretakers and custodians of the physical world. Their functions include creating the energy matrices for forms, helping them grow, preserving them and protecting them. They are also involved in weather patterns and carry out day-to-day karma for individuals incarnate on the planet.

These beings have been written about in folklore and fairy tales as fairies, elves, gnomes, nyads, dryads, sylphs, guardian angels, gods and the like, but they are all one *class* of being. They vary greatly in size and function. They are the same in essence, and interestingly, they have been identified and written about in some form in every culture, with a heavy emphasis on ancient Greek writings, which detail spirits of air, water, rivers, oceans, forests and woodlands and also describe many gods and goddesses.

Some of you may be familiar with the works of Carl Jung and know that he refers to these kinds of beings as archetypes in the collective unconscious. He also believed that fairy tales were very important to understand, which they are, because if one wants to understand the nature of these fourth-dimensional beings, one can learn a great deal from the myths and fairy tales from many cultures.

Some in this kingdom have been charged with the work of creating and maintaining the forms of nature; this refers to plants and gardens, wildernesses and forests, streams and rivers and large areas of land — even countries. Another group works with the human form and the physical and emotional bodies. Yet another group works with humans from the spiritual perspective. God and goddess forms work specifically with humans. These are embodiments of energy from the source of All That Is and are analogous to a ray of white light that has been split through a prism into seven colors. This one God and Goddess force has been split so that it manifests in the fourth dimension as seven primary god and goddess forces, and the angels and devas are under the direction of these various god- forces. It does not matter what names these forces have been given; they consist of seven male and female archetypal forces. There are others we will not deal with as yet, since the full spectrum of rays on the astral plane is actually twelve, and to further complicate things, each ray has both a god and a goddess form associated with it.

It might be of interest to add here that these beings have been identified as seven archangels from the Judeo-Christian viewpoint and as gods and goddesses in the Greco/Roman and Nordic traditions. Essentially, however, they are the same beings viewed in a different light. What identifies and interrelates them are their functions, which are protection, as symbolized by the sword; healing the sick; inspiring art, music and harmony as well as communication and technology; developing psychic abilities; teaching the ancient wisdom; and bringing messages from Source to mankind.

I wish to give you a sense that the fourth dimension is the point of conscious awareness for many beings who have many functions and are connected to the Source. These beings do not have free will as you know it; however, they are powerful beings, and they see humans incarnate on the planet either as forms or as patterns of energy and light.

The fact that a whole host of beings in the fourth dimension view you as patterns of energy and light is highly significant, since it is your levels of brightness or lack thereof that they respond to. This is something that you who incarnate on the planet have the power to affect. You may choose to make your energy field light, bright, radiant and full of ethereal colors, or else dark, muddy, cloudy and dim. You may effect changes in yourself in several ways: You may meditate on the light and draw it into your energy field; you may practice positive thinking and affirmations while also accepting and encompassing your darkness with love; and you may live your lives according to higher rules and knowledge, eliminating the dullness and darkness that is the result of envy, hatred, jealousy, malice, greed and selfishness. This is the general aim of all true religious practices — not the *only* aim, certainly, but a part of the general goals.

One of the main problems now is that so many of the world religions have been changed and perverted from the purity of the original teachings. Also, with the advancement of technology, many individuals have moved toward atheism to the point where those incarnate on the planet believe only in the reality of the third dimension and choose to live their lives in fear and self-centeredness. This does not create any great brightness of energy or spirit. In fact, by living under the illusion that you are separate from Source and having no faith in higher beings, many individuals fill their energy field with black holes and patches that represent fear, envy, malice and other dark emotions. These emotions eventually translate themselves into disease and ill health. This is inevitable, because the devas who work with and maintain the physical forms of humanity and keep them healthy are blocked wherever there are negative emotions. I would certainly not wish to see any incarnate individual blamed for suffering some terrible disease such as cancer or heart disease, because the individual is not always at fault. There may be other reasons for such an experience, such as a desire to learn from the experience, but in general, a healthy attitude of optimism and kindliness, combined with a healthy physical lifestyle, promotes good health.

In fact, the devas favor most those who are artistic and musical, who love children and animals, who are self-effacing and selfless, who have kindness and a sense of humor and who are honest, faithful, generous and good. It sounds easy enough, does it not? Yet it is extremely difficult to enter into a human body and maintain those characteristics while being born into and raised in a competitive human culture.

So you see, the planet has come to the nadir of its descent into matter and is now ascending toward the fourth dimension. This would be a long, slow process if there were not a steadily increasing body of beings in the fifth dimension who are here to facilitate an accelerated transition toward the fourth dimension. This means that all those angelic forces who inhabit the fourth dimension will have more influence and effect on your lives, and you will begin to create your own experiences through your thoughts and emotions. You create an energy field of emotionally charged thoughts around yourself, and these attract various types of devic beings who work to bring people and events of a similar vibration into your sphere of activity. This is where ideas of flow come from, where synchronous events simply happen. So the burden is on you to keep your thoughts positive and kind as the Earth accelerates to higher frequencies. As you work on keeping a positive focus, meditating and purifying your energy field, you will draw to yourself helpful devic beings and experience a greater sense of synchronicity and flow in your life.

Some of you may be familiar with books on the topic of the subconscious mind. These books frequently state that you program the subconscious with your thoughts in the form of beliefs and images, and that these are then carried out by the subconscious mind. Well, this is not actually the case. It is devic forces on the astral plane or fourth dimension that respond to clearly formed and emotionally charged thought forms in your energy field. They also work to bring you experiences that will balance and brighten your energy pattern. This is the work of certain devas who work specifically with the human kingdom.

In addition, many of you may think the human body is created out of DNA, but it is generally known and understood that the genetic codes of DNA are simply recipes for making various types of proteins. There are no instructions in DNA as to how these proteins are to be assembled to make the various forms manifest in nature. This is because all the forms manifested in nature have been created with the help of the devic kingdom using energy matrices in the fourth dimension that are made out of higher-oscillating fourth-dimensional atoms.

The devas have energy blueprints to work with. Devas help form the unborn fetus and work in the growth and development of human children, feeling as much pride in their accomplishment as human parents do. So now you can begin to understand that the devic kingdom, which creates the forms of nature, has a very personalized interest in the human form, just as they do with the animal, vegetable and mineral kingdoms.

All the work of the devas is under the direction of more powerful entities, who have been identified as gods and goddesses by various cultures and worshiped as such. These beings are clearly described in astrology as personified forces that affect human physical appearance, intellect, talents, spirituality and so on. In the framework of astrology, these forces are planets moving against a backdrop of houses that affect their influence, but in the fourth dimension they are intelligent and powerful entities that affect the tides and currents of human affairs. They can be found in the various tarot decks as archetypal figures and in the Kabbala.

For example, let us examine the goddess of the green ray and her influence. She is associated with the fourth chakra (the heart chakra) and qualities of higher love, healing, arts and crafts, fertility, childbirth, the home, abundance and sensuality. She is very much in contrast to the goddess of the indigo ray, who rules the sixth chakra (the third eye), virginity, solitude, wisdom, inner knowing, the realms of the unconscious, psychic abilities and the priestess.

These beings command a vast army of devic beings, who work with individuals in correspondence with the rays that their higher selves and personality levels incarnated on, as well as which chakras are energized. This entire picture ties in with the planetary hierarchy, because you know that members of the hierarchy anchor cosmic rays on this planet and transmit the energy through their ashrams. However, the hierarchy anchors these energies on the higher mental plane or (fifth dimension), and they are stepped down and transmitted from there to the astral plane (fourth dimension). For every devic god or goddess on the astral plane, which is primarily a level of highly charged emotion, there is a corresponding master on the mental plane who works with the same energies but from the perspective of occupations in the human sphere of activities.

Again, your material world is accelerating rapidly toward the fourth dimension, and just as you cannot always sense speed while traveling in a large vehicle, you cannot directly sense this acceleration. At this time it is important that you maintain a constant attitude of faith, hope and cheerfulness no matter what your circumstances, since your thoughts and feelings will affect your energy field on the fourth dimension and the devic beings who work on this level will have increasingly more power and influence on the physical plane.

7

Creating Prosperity

In this discussion I will explain that the goals of the majority of the world religions in the past have never been toward restructuring society or effecting change in the social order, but rather toward promising a better condition in some future state. The result of thousands of years of this type of thinking has resulted in the majority of souls coming into incarnation with the desire to experience prosperity and political freedom in contrast to past lives spent in poverty and oppression, whereas some of the most spiritually inclined souls freed themselves from the desire to be reborn and therefore were no longer incarnate. You see, in this process over time you have the more spiritually advanced souls moving out of incarnation and the most materialistic souls realizing their dreams. This condition must inevitably lead to the most unsuitable individuals having the most power over the future of the planet. Therefore I am suggesting that at this time there is a need for the most altruistic and responsible souls to acquire wealth and claim stewardship for the Earth. There is no longer a good reason to associate spirituality with poverty; rather, spirituality should be associated with unselfishness and a greater vision of the good for the greater community.

There are many ways in which one creates one's own reality. The first is by choosing the family and circumstances one will be born into. This is largely determined by strong desire in the majority of souls. The strong desire is to balance the experience of the past, so the soul in poverty and sickness yearns for a life of wealth and power, and this is the powerful force that pulls the soul back to Earth. You might say that the societies of modern America and other First World countries are the result of the endless yearnings of ancient peoples for a better life, with good health and freedom of worship and freedom from poverty and political oppression. For many souls, the desire to balance out their negative experiences is greater and more effective than any spiritual desire, and it propels them into the type of situation they seek. So the majority of souls choose their stations in life and their general circumstances, not necessarily to attain some spiritual training goal, but to attain the opposite of whatever they were experiencing in past lives. This continues until the soul gets tired and the personality begins to yearn for something different — something higher.

The first way a soul creates its own reality is by the force of desire generated by the discomforts and painful circumstances of a previous life. The soul does not come in with the intention of balancing karma, as some would have you believe, but the karma is that one situation gives rise to the yearning for its opposite.

Clearly, some of you have not come into incarnation by the force of material desire but through the force of spiritual desire. You have carefully planned the circumstances of your birth as an opportunity to grow spiritually, and you have considered what you feel you most need to learn for your spiritual growth. In the sleep state you meet with members of your spiritual family, your karmic group, and you plan when and how you will meet on the physical plane. You make changes in your basic plan while in the sleep state, but you remember nothing of this when you awake.

Now I wish to focus on the power of thought in terms of creating one's own reality on a daily basis. I would like you to imagine a person in a bubble of light as a metaphor for the mental plane. (This is not exactly the truth, only a model.) Imagine different individuals in bubbles of light. Some are dim and faint, and their light does not extend very far, whereas others are very bright and large, like the difference between a 10-watt and a 150-watt lightbulb, only more extreme. And there are individuals with various intensities of light in between. Now imagine an individual with thoughts floating around the lit bubble, like fish in a lighted aquarium. There will be abstract geometric shapes for abstract thoughts and little three-dimensional pictures for concrete thoughts, so there may be a car, a house or a beach image within the lighted sphere. These images will be colored with emotion, the pinks of love, the greens of healing and so on, and they may be kinetic and moving according to the strength of the emotion behind them.

Now I would like to describe extreme states from that of a most depraved soul to that of a most advanced soul. Imagine a very dim, murky, small light field that has small jagged geometric shapes and blurred images, with occasional flashes of red lightning and dark smoke. This would be the condition of a depraved soul. The advanced soul would have a very large, bright energy field with beautifully formed images and shapes that gracefully sail and orbit through it. Occasionally a beautifully formed thought would spin out of the field and away to perform its purpose. A beautiful geometric shape with shades of pink might take up residence in the light field of another person and exert a powerful influence there — perhaps for prosperity, healing, love and protection, based on the nature of the thought.

I wish to draw your attention to the concept that there is a combination of three principles at work. They are *thoughts from the mental body, emotions from the emotional body* and (most important) *the spiritual life force from the causal body*, which illuminates the mental field and gives power to created thoughts. Now, this is a metaphor and represents the mental energy field. But we could switch up or down levels and look at seven bodies and seven chakras and the energies coming through them. It all becomes very complicated unless you understand that there are these various levels.

Many individuals who are experiencing affluence are not necessarily adept at creating their own reality on a flexible daily basis, but are living out ancient fantasies. You who wish to change your lives must enhance your ability to use the power of thought and manifestation, which is an entirely different set of rules, so to speak. When you are limited in consciousness to the physical realm, the matter of material wealth appears to be of supreme importance, but when you are in the state between lifetimes, you are organized into many different separate realities populated by others with the same level of consciousness as yourself. Within these realities you have opportunities to meet higher beings who may come into your reality as well as ascend to their own higher-level heaven worlds. When you are in this state, if you have attained a moderate level of consciousness in which you no longer seek to balance poverty and wealth, your greatest desire then is to be more like these beings. These higher beings appear as men and women of incredible inner and outer beauty, for their inner beauty is reflected in their outward appearance. If you look within yourselves, you will find that many of you assume this to be true on the physical realm, whereas most often it is not, and many of you have been confused when meeting people of great physical beauty who do not have especially pleasant characters.

On the inner planes you cannot help but adore these higher beings and yearn to attain their level of selfless, tolerant love and compassion. What is most important to you as souls sojourning in these inner dimensions between lives is character development, not wealth. In these dimensions character is the currency that will help you attain your greatest desires. In order to join and be like these higher beings from your deepest desires, you design lifetimes that will enhance the characteristics you need most, and you do this with the help of guides and teachers. Some souls choose the option of an extremely short and painful life in a poverty-stricken Third World country because this is an opportunity to learn a great deal in a very short time.

The beauty of an incarnation on Earth is that it affords an opportunity to mix with individuals who span a range of levels of consciousness, and this interaction makes it possible to grow very quickly.

The interesting thing is that once you consciously know what you are doing while incarnated in a physical body, it is no longer necessary to take the path of pain as a means of character development. The purpose was to improve your level of love and to test it, but now you may switch to visualizing yourself filled with light. This simple practice, performed for a few minutes with other meditation practices, increases your level of tolerance, compassion, harmlessness and love by dissolving any unlike qualities. It is as if a hard shell is dissolved away to reveal who you really are.

Once you have attained a point in your life where you are self-disciplined in following the practices of a spiritual lifestyle, the level of your power increases to a great degree. Jesus said, "If thine eye be single, thy whole body shall be full of light" [Matt. 6:22]. Roughly translated, this means that if you focus on spiritual matters and self-discipline, your energy field will have a very bright soul energy. At this level of being you may sit down and form a clear thought of what you want, and it appears like a holographic image in your energy field. Writing what you wish for is a means of making a very precise thought.

At the point when you fill your energy field with clear thoughts that appear as small holographic images to those with the eyes to see, elemental beings (related to the devas) work with you and use the energy of attraction on the inner planes to bring what you wish for into your life. In the mythology of the Middle East these beings were referred to as genies or djinn (jinn). As you grow in harmlessness, compassion and love, your light becomes brighter and commands more respect from these elemental beings. It is reasonable to create a thought form for any material thing you feel you need in order to continue your mission on the Earth. If you feel you need to live in a better home, you may create a precise thought of that home for the elementals to work with. They will bring you what you need. Jesus alluded to this when he said such things as, "If you ask your father for bread, does he give you a stone? Likewise my Father in heaven will meet your needs" or something to that effect [Matt. 8:9-11]. If you ask for a car, you will get a car. If you ask for a house, you will get a house. The most important thing is to carefully and clearly write down your thoughts and imagine them in your energy field.

As you work on your spiritual development and attain higher levels of spiritual status, you will have greater power to command the elemental forces who respond to your level of light. At this stage, what prevents you from attaining your goals are countermanding thoughts that confuse the elementals, who simply follow your directions and thoughts. Any limiting thoughts such as, "This is not spiritual" or "I am not worthy" will confuse them.

The final step, of course, must be to open up channels by which the universe can bring you what you have required. You must go out into the world to meet people and perform actions that will make it possible to bring to you what you desire.

8

Shaping your Future

I have described the culture of Atlantis, and this is really our starting point for understanding what is happening in the world today. In the heyday of Atlantis, many masters walked the Earth and were accessible to share their wisdom and lives with their students and followers. The wisdom teachings of Atlantis were the purest expression of wisdom ever known and understood in the history of this planet, and they combined an essential understanding of physics and chemistry with the process of raising consciousness to higher levels.

There were seven temples that trained students in a variety of disciplines, which included science, healing, arts, music, seership, telepathy, political leadership and other fields of endeavor. After the destruction of Atlantis the masters no longer walked the Earth, and the wisdom teachings were shattered into tiny pockets of knowledge retained by small groups of survivors.

The teachings were no longer complete and the sciences were almost completely lost.

Now we have reached a time in Earth's history when many of the higher initiates from Atlantis have returned, especially those from the Temple of Science. Thus we see a sudden flowering of technology. These initiates from the Temple of Science had raised their consciousness in the past to a level from which they could tune in to the frequencies of the higher mental plane — a plane of pure understanding.

Some of you may recall that Plato wrote about this in his descriptions of Socrates. He discusses learning as a process of tuning in to a level of pure thought and archetypal essences. Well, many of the great men of science, such as Tesla and Einstein, did this. You must also understand that many of the greatest minds in mathematics and science do not have to remember a lot of facts — they just tune themselves in to the information they have learned about, which always exists on the higher mental plane, and then expand what they already know through intuitive processes, much like channeling.

Perhaps in your more outlandish science fiction you have come upon the idea of specialized areas of the brain that are accessible only to geniuses. Actually, this is somewhat true, for such people have developed the mechanisms of the higher chakras, which allows access to the higher mental plane. This gift was usually developed in past lives.

With the ongoing work on the inner planes of raising the level of frequency on the planet with the help of all those groups who meditate on sending light through the etheric web, the planet is becoming more infused with energies that are accelerating the Earth toward the fourth and fifth dimension. With each passing day it becomes more and more possible for individuals to tune themselves in to these higher levels of the mental plane, which we refer to as the fifth dimension. It is also becoming increasingly true that the thoughts you have in your minds are shaping your personal reality. This message is coming from ever more channels and teachers.

Many of you may feel some skepticism toward the idea that thoughts shape reality — some resistance and even an unwillingness to accept such a belief. Certainly it has often been presented in a way that has not been easy to comprehend, with a heavy emphasis on the idea that beliefs shape reality. It is not so much your beliefs, but the *totality* of your beliefs, thoughts and imaginings that shape your reality. You must learn to use the concentrated focus of your will to shape a positive reality for the future, which means that you must have goals and that you must eradicate beliefs that interfere with your goals. You must frequently use the power of your imagination to picture positive outcomes and devote some time to imagining yourself living your positive future.

In order to do this, it is sometimes helpful to review your life and remember how things may have been going well when a mood of pessimism, self-hatred, feelings of worthlessness or a belief in the inevitability of suffering caused things to take a turn for the worse. Remember a time when you were motivated to attain some goal and you did it. Did you believe that because you were on the spiritual path your accumulated bad karma would be dumped on you? This is not true, and you do not have to suffer further karma.

It is time to remember who you are and become the

magician, creator, wizard and master that you are and demonstrate that you can create a wonderful reality for yourself. Decide right now that you are here to learn the lessons that accompany prosperity, positive and healthy relationships, the expression of your greatest gifts and talents and travel to exotic places. Allow yourself to have this. Allow yourself to live on a planet of peace, harmony and wisdom, without pollution. This is your major task at this time, and you will see this same information come through channel after channel. Realize that the greatest service you can perform for the planet at this time is this work of imagining a positive future for yourself and all others.

I am telling you that one of the greatest acts of service you may perform is to imagine a positive future for Earth. This is what Gene Roddenberry did when he created *Star Trek*. He implanted such a vision in the collective consciousness of mankind. Consider that before the advent of the *Star Trek* television series, most people imagined that the planet would be destroyed in a nuclear holocaust. Gene Roddenberry imagined the most positive future he could, and he made it into a television series that planted this concept into the minds of the viewing audience. If you understand that thoughts and expectations shape reality, you will see what a valuable service he performed.

I also wish you to disregard all possible scenarios that include asteroids crashing into the planet, overpopulation causing starvation, a millennium bug causing widespread devastation or an invasion of hostile aliens. You are being presented with such visions everywhere you turn, and this is not the time to be entertaining such ideas. Hold firmly a vision of the best possible outcomes in all areas.

Remember what I have told you: Thoughts create thought forms, and these thought forms have an atomic structure in the fifth dimension. Remember that everything in this third-dimensional reality of yours has an electrically charged energy matrix on the higher dimensions. When you hear so many teachers talking about light and light work, remember that the structures on the inner planes are luminous and composed of radiant atoms. Light takes form on the inner planes. There is no separation between spirit and matter, and higher beings are not formed by light as you know it, but are made up of luminous matter, tangible on those dimensions.

If you were suddenly transported to the fifth dimension where I dwell, you would see me as a lightbeing, but you would be able to feel me as a solid energy entity. You would also see that I dwell in a house in a beautiful location high up in the mountains and that all the objects in my house have their own inner radiance. Atoms having higher atomic frequency than the atoms of your dimension emit light. All atoms are electrical in their essence and have either a positive charge, which is magnetic and attracting, or a negative charge, which repels. Breaking the bond between electrons and neutrons releases energy in the form of light and heat.

The universe is a complex arrangement of formed electricities and formless energies. Where there are atoms, there is electrical energy. Atoms and subatomic particles shape the entire universe and the inner planes as well. Using your mind to shape this high-energy electrical light matter into your future is your gift, and this is what you are here to learn to do.

There is a difference between the lower mind and the higher mind, which might be differentiated as the ego and the illumined mind. The ego has developed in humanity because the vast majority of you have been raised in a spirit of false religions and lies that have given you a profound sense of isolation from All That Is. With this isolation has come the extreme development of the negative ego, which exists to preserve itself and has a specific nature of its own.

Those forces that have forever sought to enslave humanity in ignorance and despair have created the conditions that maintain the negative ego and all the ills accompanying it. This was intentional, since negative emotions generated from the type of thinking native to the ego can be used and harnessed as a kind of powerful energy. These forces wishing to enslave mankind work ceaselessly to program you with ideas that promote feelings of pain, despair, judgment, envy, jealousy, malice and rage. Now it is time to see through the illusion and focus your mind on the higher mental plane. More help will be made available to you if you ask for it. Your guides, teachers and helpers will become increasingly more real to you and offer practical help in the form of nudges and reminders, inspirations and insights, encouraging you to become calm and meditate on the light — and daydream.

9

The Arthurian Legend

There is a lot of interest at this time in the Arthurian legend and the symbols associated with it, as well as other closely related stories involving the knights of the Round Table, the Holy Grail, and the story of the Grail King.

This mythology originated on the continent of Atlantis and much earlier than had been thought. I would estimate that Atlantis existed from 24,000 to 12,000 years ago. It is an amazing notion that the mythology of an Atlantean warrior king called Arthur has existed and been passed along for such a long time, emerging with great force in the 8th, 9th 10th and 11th centuries.

As I have said before, the people of Atlantis varied in type from north to south. The northern portion of Atlantis was very much like northern Europe or Canada because it was an area of forests, rivers and lakes, with open meadows and a temperate climate that had cold winters. The people who lived in the northern part of Atlantis found that they could function and think clearly only in such a climate. When they moved toward the warmer regions nearer the equator, they developed all kinds of illnesses and diseases. They did not feel well. The sun burned their skin and they developed sunstroke and skin cancers. Their minds became unclear and confused, almost like symptoms of dementia. They were the ancestors of Europeans and the people of northern India.

The people of the southern part of Atlantis lived in a flat, pleasant land that had the characteristics of tropical regions, such as wide, white sandy beaches, palm trees and blue lagoons, with inland swamps and rain forests. They were a darker people, and were the ancestors of the oriental and Native American peoples, including South American natives. Both types of people had mutated from an original Lemurian type. They mutated under the conditions of Atlantis, which was a complicated process related to changes produced in the DNA by the Sun's radiation that varied according to latitude.

There were people in the middle area of Atlantis who were not especially one type or another, but a blend. They had light skin and dark hair or light skin and red hair. They resembled what you would consider Mediterranean and Celtic peoples.

There were temples of the Order of Melchizedek all over Atlantis; there were seven different orders but more than seven temples. Each order had a specific symbol, and the symbols had many meanings. They included a large golden cup, a sword of power, a spear of power, a gold pentacle, a gold ring, a cauldron or bowl and a staff of power. These are the things that magic is made of. These symbols are associated with the seven rays and represent the seven dimensions and the major quality associated with each. The four basic symbols of the pentacle, the wand, the sword and the cup appear in the tarot cards and correspond to Earth, water, air and fire as well as the physical, emotional, mental and soul planes. Over time they evolved into the suits in regular playing cards — diamonds, hearts, clubs and spades.

Briefly speaking, the gold coin with a five-pointed star is the symbol for the third dimension, which can sometimes be abbreviated to the symbol of a *five-pointed star*. This symbol is associated with the physical plane, the base chakra, the first ray, the color red and the element of Earth. It has evolved into money in the form of gold coins.

The *spear* or *wand* is associated with the second ray, the second chakra , the element of water, and control over the emotions. The *sword* is associated with the mental plane, the third chakra, the intellect and the element of air. The *cup* is associated with the fourth chakra, the soul plane, the healing energies of the heart, the fourth ray of healing and the arts. The remaining symbols are associated with the remaining rays and higher chakras, which are briefly: a *ring* with the fifth ray, a *cauldron* with the sixth ray, and the seventh ray can be symbolized by either a *crown* or a *staff* of power.

What is interesting about these symbols is that they are featured in all of the most profound stories and myths relating to the spiritual path and the ordeals of the individual who is walking it. You may examine the life of Jesus and see that many of the symbols are featured in his life and that many of these same symbols reappear in the story of Arthur, who is seeking the holy cup, the grail, the fourth initiation — the crucifixion and the power associated with it.

At the time of the sinking of Atlantis and Earth cat-
aclysms, groups of priests and priestesses from the various orders escaped in flying vehicles with the physical
symbols. Most of these symbols had some sort of
properties that one might consider magical, but that
were actually an advanced technology.

When all these groups found themselves split up and
divided around the planet, some had the temple symbols
and some did not. All sorts of stories arose, and many
groups made various attempts to find these articles.

The most significant fact of this entire work is that
in the most ancient teachings — the Indian Vedas, the
Judaic texts (which emerged out of ancient Egyptian
philosophy), the Bible, astrology, the tarot and the mythology of the Greeks, Romans, Celts and Native
Americans — are embedded symbols, myths and illus-
trative stories originating in the mystical orders of
Atlantis that share a common thread. All these symbolic images and stories refer to the different dimensions, the devic and god forces and the journey of the
soul through life in this illusory third dimension.

Many fragmentary groups escaping from Atlantis
left monuments that illustrated their advanced technology. The ancient Egyptians had all sorts of devices and
symbols, and they built the Sphinx and the pyramids
by employing these devices after the sinking of
Atlantis.

Thus these symbols had high technology built into
them, and they were symbols for the various orders as
well.

The mythology of King Arthur was based around a
wise, mythological ruler who supposedly lived during
the latter days of Atlantis and who created the concept
of a round table of local rulers where no one was more

important than another and also created rules of conduct for warriors. Those who escaped from Atlantis to colonies that had been set up in the British Isles and northern Europe brought the mythology of the Arthurian legend with them. Of course, over thousands of years the legend has become somewhat mixed up and confused, but, like the story of Jesus, it illustrates the path of initiation or the journey of the human soul in incarnation. This particular myth is a story from the order of the First Ray.

It was generally thought that after the destruction of Atlantis, the followers of the order related to Arthur made it to safety in the British Isles, which was a colony of north Atlantis. They brought the symbol of the Temple of Intelligent Activity, the *golden sword*, with them. The other symbols were lost, but some of them made their way to the British Isles at a later time. Special protective forces were set up around the British Isles at the time of the destruction of Atlantis, and these forces lay dormant for thousands of years until the time of Queen Elizabeth I's astrologer John Dee found magical means to reactivate the protective forces around the British Isles. Some of these means included invoking the cooperation of the sea gods, who have a dual role of protecting the mysteries and protecting the British Isles. So the impossible act of sinking the Spanish Armada became a reality, and Britain emerged as a world power that was based on its navy.

For 12,000 years of Earth history groups have come into being to search for and find these powerful sacred symbols, and there have been groups that built temples in which to guard and hide these symbols. Secretly, beneath the wars and crusades throughout history, there has been one group of people trying to steal these symbols from another.

The important issue here is that these objects need to be in the hands of those forces aligned to goodness and truth rather than those that would oppress humanity. So it has always been a battle for the powers of good to wrest these objects from those who would abuse their power.

Since ancient times the British Isles have been considered holy isles, and several of these symbolic objects were brought there to be hidden and protected. Other sacred objects were hidden in Tibet. Moses stole some of these objects from the Egyptians and took them to Israel in a container he called the Ark of the Covenant. Throughout history wars were fought to obtain these objects, and secret orders were formed to hide and protect them. Among them were antigravity devices that made it possible to move gigantic pieces of rock. There were laser- type devices that made it possible to easily cut straight slabs of rock. There were cornucopia-like devices that manufactured food out of almost nothing. There were objects that conferred power on their owners. The sword Excalibur is such an object. There were also weapons of horrifying, destructive power.

These objects are somewhere in the world today, guarded by whatever groups have them in safekeeping. The images and symbols associated with these myths and legends have a great deal of potency on the astral planes. They are related to the elements, the various levels of dimensions and the seven rays. Those who perform ritual magic use their own personal versions of these symbols in their rituals in order to invoke various forces. They invoke the elemental forces of the astral plane.

Invoking the symbols of Arthur draws the attention of those on the inner planes who work in the associated temples related to those objects and the rays associated with them. You have a lot to ponder if you are familiar with the symbology used in occult, magical and wiccan thought.

In particular, astrology references the planets as rulers of certain signs, and these are given the attributes of the Greek and Roman gods. These archetypal figures represented Roman gods originating in the Atlantean religion as the lords of the rays. Again, without going into too much depth, we have the Warrior King (Mars), who represents the first ray, the red ray of intent. There is the Sun/Son God/Charioteer (Apollo), who represents the second ray of Love/Wisdom, the purified emotions. There is the Messenger/Trickster/Magician (Mercury), who represents the power of the mind, the third ray. The fourth ray, that of arts and healing, is represented by a goddess figure — the love Goddess/Empress (Venus), who presides over abundance, beauty, the home and arts and crafts. The fifth ray, that of telepathy, communication and harmonies, corresponds to the Hermit (Saturn), The sixth ray of devotion and the monadic plane corresponds to the Moon Goddess/Virgin/Priestess (Moon). The seventh ray of ceremonial magic corresponds to the Wise Old Man/Hierophant/Pope (Jupiter). These same characters appear in other mythologies with different names, such as in the life of Jesus and the story of Arthur and his knight Percival.

Certain archetypal characters and symbols appear frequently in various cultures, acting in various roles and describing the journey of the hero or candidate on the path of initiation. There is a universal language of symbology in unrelated cultures that is a remnant of the one religion of Atlantis.

10

The Language of Mythology

I am proposing a theory that the basic mystery teach-ings, as they were presented on the continent of Atlantis, can be found in the mythology of many cul-tures and that there is a key to the interpretation of these mysteries in both astrology and the tarot cards.

I suggest that the rulers of the rays, the god forces on the inner planes that are also the consciousnesses of the planets, appear in mythology as archetypal entities — sometimes as gods and sometimes as kings and queens. These same rulers of the rays appear in astrol-ogy as the planetary rulers, which are the Sun, Moon, Mercury, Venus, Mars, Jupiter, Saturn, Pluto, Neptune and Uranus. Of course, there are ten planetary rulers, but some of them double up on one ray (and the Sun and Moon are not planets, of course). These planets are accorded traits that correspond to the characteristics of the Greco-Roman gods of the same name. Thus there are archetypal beings from Greco-Roman mythology who are a warrior king, charioteer, messenger, trickster, virgin huntress or priestess, queen, hermit, magician, king of the underworld, king of the seas and inventor or blacksmith. These beings appear also in the tarot deck as similar archetypal characters. So archetypal characters appear in the tales and mythologies of all cultures, and there are goals to be attained and objects to be acquired. These symbolic objects represent the attainment of higher and higher levels of consciousness. By using the tarot and astrology as keys to understand symbolism, we can recognize the correspondences between objects and levels of consciousness. The suits of the tarot — pentacles, wands, swords and cups — correspond to the elements of Earth, air, fire and water that appear in astrology and can also be represented by the fixed signs, which are the lion, the bull, the eagle and the water-bearing human.

Also, the **physical realm** can be related to the bull, Earth and the pentacle (the five-pointed star). The **astral plane or fourth dimension** can be related to the eagle, water and the wand. The **mental plane** can be represented by the water bearer, air and swords. The **causal plane** can be represented by the lion, fire and cups. The elements also relate to the phases of birth, baptism, temptation and crucifixion.

The Mythical Journey

In the folk tales of many cultures we find characters and objects that describe the mythical journey of a hero to attain a goal, and this is the story of everyman, or perhaps everysoul, in a certain sense.

The ancient Greek structure for dramatic productions emerged out of the sacred rituals of the many Mediterranean pagan cults, rituals that were performed in secret for their initiates. In similar fashion the ancient Celtic cults acted out ritual stories that appear, upon superficial examination, to have some relationship to the progression of the four seasons. But it is the other way around, and the seasons of birth, death and rebirth are a reminder of the spiritual cycles. In the Greek dramatic tradition there are certain characters such as the protagonist, antagonist, nemesis and love interest, each of whom have a prescribed role to play in the drama. This structure has remained fairly consistent throughout the Western dramatic tradition and harks back to the mystery tradition in which the antagonist, nemesis and love interest represent facets of the candidate for initiation that must be integrated into the personality.

Every good, classic legend that has its roots in the mystery tradition begins with a miraculous *birth* of a miraculous child. The miracle child or hero/heroine represents everysoul, and usually the parentage is both human and divine or human and royal, signifying that humanity is both human and limited and divine and unlimited. Often the true identity of the child is not revealed until further on in the legend as the hero/heroine displays superhuman attributes. This event represents the first initiation along the path, when the conscious self gains control of the physical body.

All humanity has attained this to a basic degree, inasmuch as all of you are functional within your reality. But there are more refined levels of self-discipline, which confer upon the initiate radiant physical health and youthful appearance into old age. This stage is the beginning of the spiritual journey where the self makes a conscious decision to live according to spiritual principles.

The next phase in a good classical initiatory path or mystery legend is that of *baptism* by water, which signifies becoming connected to a teaching tradition and a teacher or mentor who will work with the candidate on attaining compassion and emotional control. This can be symbolized by feats such as walking on water, being ritualistically immersed in water or surviving a terrible storm at sea.

In the third phase or aspect of a mystery legend, the hero is tempted (the *temptation*) to misuse his magical or superhuman powers for his own benefit. In a simpler story this is symbolized by acquiring a magical sword that can be used only for good, lest it destroy the one who wields it. This corresponds to the third initiation, which is that of gaining control of the mind and overcoming the negative ego.

The fourth phase in a mystery legend is the *crucifixion*, which may be represented as the death of an old personality and the rebirth into a new way of being or as experiencing a betrayal that requires forgiveness. Themes for this phase are sacrifice and forgiveness and the opening of the heart chakra (the source of healing energies), symbolized by the Holy Grail. In a simpler story this stage may be represented by the hero fighting a lion, which relates to the constellation Leo. In astrology Leo is connected to the element of fire and the fourth initiation.

The fifth phase of the universal story is the *transfiguration*, whereby the new personality is unrecognizable to those who know him. This represents the fifth initiation, which is the initiation in which the candidate becomes a master in his own right. It is the beginning of control of the three higher chakras, which relate to group goals, telepathy, psychic powers and mystical union with God. The throat chakra is activated, which relates to telepathy and communication. This level is control of the buddhic plane, and a ring of power is the object to be obtained.

The sixth phase is that of *resurrection.* This can be likened to a recovery from a lingering illness or a literal revival from death. This corresponds to the third-eye chakra and psychic powers that are awakened on attaining this initiation. This corresponds to the atmic plane and a gold crown with jewels in it.

The final stage is that of the *ascension,* which may be told in myth as the disappearance of the hero, with the assurance that he will return when needed at some future time. Objects associated with this level are the gold scepter or rod of power with a diamond at the tip.

So you see that the hidden or secret mystery teachings from Atlantis are already familiar to you and that you have already been taught about the seven initiations the human soul undergoes. You have also learned about the rulers of the rays, who influence the candidate for initiation. All this has been given to you in the ancient stories of Hercules, Jesus, Arthur, Percival and other heroes. Incidently, I am not saying that Jesus was not a real person, but rather that he lived out the classical life of the initiate.

Now I would like to address those great works of children's fiction that lead the reader into inner realms of fantasy and imagination — those in which objects such as trees, flowers and animals can talk to the hero/heroine, suggesting that the author is tapping into the fourth dimension and describing the characteristics of that dimension in fictional form. Whether the realm is called Wonderland, Middle Earth, Narnia or the Land of Oz, these fantasy realms have certain aspects in common and represent different levels and localities of the fourth dimension that reflect the collective unconscious of European peoples. Within these fantasy lands there is also often a battle going on between the forces of light and dark, good and evil, innocence and corruption. The author must create a suitable hero/heroine whose main characteristic is usually innocence, purity and compassion. Often that main character is a girl child, the archetypal symbol of human innocence and purity. This girl child must venture into this realm to save the Earth by obtaining a magical object that sways the balance in favor of the forces of light, or she must gain some insight that reality is but an illusion. Writing this epic and distributing it to the population adds strength to the inner-plane reality that the author has tapped into and to the forces of good. The release of such a fiction to the reading public during a period of national trial has a strengthening and reviving effect on the spirit of the nation.

11

The Ascension Process

In this discussion on the nature of the coming changes and their relation to the fourth and fifth dimensions, I would like to touch upon the theme of the ascension process, since it is being presented to you through many different sources and teachers. Some of you are familiar with the older theosophical teachings dispensed at the end of the last century and the beginning of this century. There was a heavy emphasis on the path of initiation and the path of discipleship, and many ideas expressed in those books were influenced by both the Hindu religion and the mystery school tradition, which were both remnants of the Atlantean religion.

There were many mystery school and occult traditions that required vows of secrecy, and by progressing their members through different levels of initiation, they were able to attain ever higher initiations within the orders. The Theosophists believed that there were cosmic mysteries and initiations and that souls in in-carnation might experience various levels of initiation in their daily lives that prepared them to take a cosmic initiation.

They also framed these concepts within an under-standing that the bulk of humanity would soon pass the third initiation, but that there was a small group of more advanced souls who were going for their fourth and fifth. This is no longer representative of the bigger picture, since many souls are coming in who have taken, or who will soon take, their fourth and fifth. It is more a matter of consolidating past attainments.

The ascension process is now being offered instead of the concept of initiation levels. It is basically the same thing with a different name. However, it should be understood that whatever we call this process, it is a process of raising the levels of personal consciousness through the planes or dimensions. In essence this means that if I have complete mastery over my emo-tions, I have raised my consciousness to the mental level. If I have complete mastery over the lower mind (the negative ego, which always feels separate from and better or worse than all other beings), I have raised my consciousness to the higher mental level, the level of pure abstract thought. When I have control of the higher mental level, then I have raised my conscious-ness to the level of the soul or higher self, that part of the Self which is one with all other selves.

Each time complete mastery is gained over a level from the physical through the emotional, the ego and the abstract mental, another initiation is attained. Now, we can symbolize these levels as Earth, water, air and fire in that order. Also, the 3D, 4D and 5D can be rep-resented as having the qualities of Earth, water, air and fire, with both air and fire representing the lower and higher levels of the 5D. So in one system we may use these symbols, or we may use the pattern from the life of the Christ as the birth, the baptism, the temptation and the crucifixion as well as the transfiguration, resurrection and ascension. We may think in terms of the kundalini serpent fire energy rising up through the base, the second, the third and the fourth chakras, but however we frame it conceptually, it is a universal process of attaining self-mastery and raising consciousness. The goal is for the higher self, located in the sixth dimension, to have complete control over the threefold personality.

The early steps on the path of initiation or ascension involve maintaining a healthy lifestyle, which is fairly basic and simple. The beginning of the path involves taking care of the physical vehicle with the proper diet (high in vegetables, grains and fruit and low in red meat), abstinence from drugs and alcohol, cleanliness, exercise, work and rest. These are also the basics of a monastic life. It also includes a balanced sexuality in a healthy relationship, or else no sex in no relationship. However, in this materialistic and hollow modern society you have only to look around to see that most others around you are struggling with some sort of out-of-control, compulsive behavior regarding the physical vehicle.

At the same time, an early stage of the path is that of studying many books to become wiser. As you get a clearer sense of order in the universe from study or from listening to teachers and lecturers, your consciousness naturally rises. You might say that my particular soul orientation is especially focused on teaching the ancient wisdom, because I am committed to the

concept that learning automatically raises consciousness. When an individual learns and accepts the true
nature of reality as presented through the wisdom
teachings, the process of developing a higher level of
consciousness occurs naturally. When the beauty and
harmony of the greater picture is viewed and understood in its entirety, it is not possible to go backward
in consciousness.

These are the beginning steps on the path, and by
following these simple steps and meditating on a daily
basis, the light an individual radiates on the inner
planes begins to increase. When the aspiring candidate's light is bright enough, the candidate joins an
ashram of one of the masters on the inner planes. The
candidate learns many things in the sleep state and usually remembers nothing in the waking state, but begins
to express in waking life some of the ideas learned in
the sleep state, perhaps to search for answers in the material world.

Meditation

Now to the topic of meditation. Because it is a crucial tool in the process, the early stages should include
quieting the mind and observing the thoughts that
arise. There should be no effort to stop them, but
rather to detach from them and view them as having a
life of their own apart from one's own personal will
and intent. It will become apparent that thoughts are
difficult to control because they have a life of their
own. In the early stages of meditation it is important to
watch the thoughts passively and frequently in order to
develop a clear distinction between the "I" and one's
thoughts. When detachment is attained, it is possible
to change your thoughts by saying to oneself, "This is a

negative thought; I will think the exact opposite instead," thus replacing it.

This is a very important technique to learn, since you will observe that your emotions and feelings follow your thoughts, and through constant vigilance you will learn how to replace the type of thoughts that generate anger, hostility, envy, rage and depression with calm thoughts that produce calm emotions. When you find yourself thinking a negative thought, ask yourself if the very opposite thought is not equally true.

While many of you pride yourselves on having your own minds and sense of reality, your thoughts are like birds flying in through an open window and flying out again. They are not actually your own; they are a frequency of mental transmission you have habitually tuned in to. So it becomes important to break free from the programming that assaults you daily through the news media and learn how you have been shaped by your upbringing in terms of class values and patriotism. Learn to view yourself as a soul in incarnation using a personality vehicle; see yourself as a citizen of the universe.

The most crucial ascension leap at this time is to make the transition to the fourth initiation, that of Christ consciousness, through the activated heart center, which is attained from living in a state of oneness and inclusiveness toward all life forms. When you can constantly monitor your thoughts and tune your mind like a radio to frequencies of love, wisdom and optimism, you are well on your way. (On you way to what?, you may wonder.)

You hear over and over again that it is important, crucial and even necessary to embody love, yet the word "love" has become so overworked in the English language that it has virtually become meaningless and incomprehensible. When we exhort you to love, what do we want of you? The first step toward embodying the consciousness of love (the Christ consciousness and the consciousness of the higher self) is to slay the personal ego. I use a metaphorical image. It is a process of monitoring the thoughts and realizing that your thoughts are not your own; they are not you. They are a frequency you have tuned in to as well as a lifetime of programming from parents, teachers, ministers, radio, television, books, movies and newspapers — a process of observation.

This process of slaying the personal ego and breaking free from programming is attained by daily meditation, which may take many forms. The first step should be *self-observation*. In this process of observing your thoughts and substituting more positive ones, you will gain control over them as well as your emotions.

Other steps along the path include visualizing different colors of light, then flooding your body with them. White, violet and gold light are the most frequently used, although we recommend white to begin with. Emptying the mind and focusing on a flame or on slow, steady breathing is the next step — *concentration*.

Focusing attention on a teaching and meditating on it comes after the mind has been emptied. Once these basic steps have been achieved, it is possible to work with progressive visualizations using the language of symbols and light to raise the frequency of your atoms.

A little time in meditation goes a long way. It is like taking a spiritual shower. Just as you are in the habit of jumping into your shower for a few minutes to immerse yourself in purifying water, so you should mentally jump into the light and feel light washing through you for a few minutes at the beginning or end of each day, washing negative thoughts and emotions away. It is not necessary to engage in long, complicated meditations — daily short meditations will suffice. The highest state of attainment is to be in a state of meditation throughout the day while performing mundane tasks.

Now, the process of taking these initiations will come in the form of passing tests and trials in everyday life that will substantiate that the individual has learned the lesson associated with a particular level of consciousness. For each initiation there is a keynote, a quality that must be demonstrated, such as self-discipline, harmlessness, humility, forgiveness, kindness, tolerance and discrimination. These opportunities come daily in dealing with coworkers and family members.

However, the greatest task facing many souls in incarnation at this time is that of transcending the personal ego. This has been the major focus of many Eastern disciplines such as Buddhism and Zen Buddhism. The experience called enlightenment is actually what Theosophists would call the third initiation, that of the temptation. At this point, having gained enlightenment, the initiate knows that he or she is one in consciousness with everything in the universe.

A Separate Personal Identity

The consciousness of many souls is stuck in a strong sense of separate personal identity, personal accomplishments, aims and desires, with powerful ego boundaries designed to keep others at an emotional distance — to keep them "in their place." Nothing feeds more strongly into the concept of personal ego than that of rank or status and a general sense of being better than or different from others.

This process begins early in childhood when individuals are socialized by the culture they are born into. They develop a sense of self, and this sense of self develops in terms of being better than or inferior to others. With a sense of superiority, now called positive self-esteem, the ego grows. The isolated ego can always find ways to prove its own superiority, or in some cases to defend its sense of inferiority. The ego is, by its very nature, opposed to the expression of love. It is from the ego mind that the desire stems to make others wrong — the desire to criticize, argue, ridicule, belittle, deride, prove a point and make comparisons between the self and others. This ego mind must be mastered, transcended and filled with the illumination of the higher self. At this point it becomes the illumined mind.

If each infant soul had been born into a society that taught the ancient wisdom teachings, it would be an easy matter to breeze through the initiation process. But in the industrialized world, individuals are heavily programmed by scientific materialism, a religion in itself, which shapes the individual's sense of reality. In many cultures in the past there were temple systems that took a few individuals through a process of initiation. However, in the past hundred years, scientific materialism, with its dazzling display of technological wizardry, has converted many into skeptics and atheists. And since many of the existing world religions contain only a small portion of the truth and are mainly distortions of the truth, it is not a bad idea to break free of their insidious programming by becoming an atheist for a limited of time.

The Social Self

Other problems of early social conditioning are those of developing a sense of the social self in terms of status in society and loyalty to your birth nation. A true sense of personal self-worth should be based on attaining skills and accomplishments rather than a feeling of superiority that originates from factors such as gender, nationality or race.

The oriental religions, such as Zen, have focused basically on deprogramming the individual from the many layers of social conditioning that have fostered the development of a strong personal ego. When after much effort the student bursts free of the limits of the ego, which is like a container, the student experiences a sense of mystical union with all life. This is the process of attaining the third initiation.

The focus of the fourth initiation is that of personal sacrifice and forgiveness toward those who persecute. The Master Jesus prepared his followers for this initiation, and many biblical quotes illustrate the theme "Bless those who curse you" and "Turn the other cheek," to name two. At this initiation the heart chakra becomes activated with a flow of healing green energy from the fourth ray. For the individual immersed in taking this initiation, life may be very difficult, calling for many sacrifices and coping with constant persecutions.

The Merkaba

You may have heard of the merkaba vehicle in channeled writings from various sources and wonder what it is. Picture in your mind a pyramid of light and above it an inverted pyramid of light. The bottom pyramid of light represents the personality self, composed of body, emotions and mind. The upper triangle represents the higher self, composed of causal, buddhic, atmic and monadic energy matrices. As the conscious self gains greater control of the personality, the two pyramids slowly move toward each other and merge into what might be described as a three-dimensional Star of David inside an energy sphere. This is the merkaba. This is to some degree the goal of the initiation process. As the kundalini fire moves up through the chakras and stabilizes at higher chakras, the two energy fields of the merkaba move closer together and merge. It takes many lifetimes to attain this completed energy field, and it is no small accomplishment.

At this time many teachers are offering workshops in the ascension process. There is no harm in this, but remember that the real ascension process is in the tests and trials of daily life, whereby you are tested continually to see how suitable you are for gaining greater power. This is the major significance of Sanat Kumara, in that he has made Earth a school of initiation, and that initiation comes through the ordinary trials of dealing with family and coworkers. You do not need to join some mystical organization. You do not need to do complicated exercises. You need to rid yourself of selfish aims and desires and prove through your actions that you have attained a certain degree of selflessness.

12

Some Thoughts on Channeling

I would like to discuss some thoughts on the process of channeling. Many of you may read the diverse messages that have been brought through by many channels and feel some skepticism when you notice either that the channels agree on many ideas or that, conversely, they disagree considerably.

I would like to describe this process to you from my vantage point as an energy being who exists in consciousness in the fifth dimension, or what used to be referred to as the higher levels of the abstract mental plane. I am a part of a planetary hierarchy of human souls who have attained a level of self-mastery throughout many lifetimes. I took the bodhisattva vow to remain on this planet, but many souls have chosen to continue learning and growing on other planets in other dimensions and use the gifts that were developed in this hard school of the third dimension. This particular school of spiritual development is in the process of being closed down, renovated and changed from the metaphorical level of an elementary school to that of a university.

When Helena Blavatsky began her mission on Earth as founder of the Theosophical Society, only a handful of masters revealed themselves to her. And Alice Bailey, a theosophical student, listed and described perhaps twelve or so. At this time in Earth's history, the numbers and ranks of masters on the inner planes are swelling daily as more and more lightbeings flock here to aid in the transition of the planet from a third-dimensional school to a fourth- and then a fifth-dimensional planet. You may know that I am technically known as a master of the Second Ray, which means that I receive and transmit a particular type of cosmic energy.

Now many are joining me and working with me in anchoring this energy on the inner planes and are also working with other members of the planetary hierarchy to anchor the six other cosmic rays. So there is a growing group of master teachers and angelic hosts who may describe themselves under a variety of names. But what we have in common is that we exist as energy beings on the fifth dimension and we follow the details of a divine plan for the destiny of this tiny turquoise planet, who is herself a spiritual being with a consciousness and who is also overlighted by the presence of Sanat Kumara, the Planetary Logos.

So all of us here are of one accord and one mind, whether we are Arcturians, Seth, Ramtha, Pleiadians, ascended masters of the human planetary round, archangels, devas or the Ashtar Command. We are all telepathic beings who reside in the fifth dimension.

Part of the work we have undertaken to perform requires lightworkers in the third dimension to work with some of us telepathically in order to release teachings to the world. Such individuals have come to be known as channels. If you are one who has followed the esoteric teachings of the past, you will have noticed that there was a progression to the concepts that were revealed to the populace. The ancient wisdom teachings were released in a sequence of concepts. When these individuals channeled and published their works, the conditions of the planet were much denser and lower in frequency than they are now, and mistakes were made. But the bulk of the teachings served to form a language of concepts upon which we might build.

I might stop here to use an analogy from the computer technology that abounds today. When you wish to download a file from another computer, it is necessary to have some sort of program in the receiving computer that can translate that file. It might be a word processing program or an Internet viewer, but whatever it is, it will have been distributed by a company that distributes millions of identical copies.

You are all like computers that have created your own software programs. The data in your memory banks is not identical for any two of you. Since infancy you have been amassing and storing data in the form of language and concepts, and although there may be overlapping areas of knowledge, no two of you share the exact same database. This is very different from the computer world, where identical database software can be obtained to make computers compatible. You may imagine that you all share the same language, but problems arise between you in terms of miscommunication, because each of you defines each word a little differently in terms of subtle shades of meaning and concept.

From esoteric understanding, your memories are not stored in your brains, as you suppose, but in a magnetic energy field called the reflecting ether. Science has gained some understanding of the brain by stimulating various parts of it with electricity while the subject is conscious, learning which memories are awakened, and by studying people with damage to various parts of the brain. But science does not understand how memories can be stored in the neurons of the brain — and this is because *they are not.* Everything you have ever read or experienced is stored in a field of energy that you often refer to as the subconscious mind. This term "subconscious" emerged out of the field of hypnosis and suggestion and the idea that memories exist below the threshold of consciousness. This field of research greatly influenced men like Sigmund Freud, who coined the term "unconscious mind."

So from the perspective of those of us in the fifth dimension, the best channels are those who have been exposed to a great variety of concepts, especially esoteric concepts, so that we share a compatible program, so to speak. If we wish to transmit a concept that absolutely does not exist in the subconscious energy field of the channel, it will not register in the conscious mind at all. When this is the case, we can use metaphors and analogies, but discrepancies may yet occur. One of the problems with finding a suitable personality to use as a channel of the wisdom teachings is that individuals raised in families and a society that have imposed a heavy conditioning program on them at an early age may produce biases in their energy fields that warp the incoming transmissions. It is analogous to attempting to shine a white light through tinted glass. The personality of the channel colors the message.

What we are attempting to do is present the information as a jigsaw puzzle wherein many channels have one or two pieces of the bigger picture; and when the totality of the channeled transmissions are viewed together, the bigger picture emerges. Sometimes we give the same piece to many channels so that confirmation arises independently. Sometimes a channel completely misunderstands a transmission, making it quite inaccurate. However, as the frequency of the planet is being raised by carefully regulated surges of energy through the etheric grid, more and more individuals are opening their inner ears and eyes, and channeled messages will become more and more numerous from a greater variety of channels. So my suggestion to you is that you make your own inner contacts with your guides and teachers and study the published materials to see where they agree with your inner sense of knowing.

It will not be necessary in the days ahead for individuals to go into a trance state and lose conscious memory of what was said while in trance. The safest and most accurate method of channeling is a conscious, clairaudient state, whereby the channel mentally hears the message in his or her own voice, since the incoming thoughts are translated into words in their subconscious energy field, and then the channel writes these thoughts down. I would recommend that you find a quiet place where you can go into a meditative state, then ask your higher self for protection. State the name of the being you wish to contact and if possible, look at a painting or sketch of this entity prior to attempting this so that you can form a mental image of the entity. The process of sounding the name and having a mental image is like having the correct telephone number of a person you are trying to call. It is a means of establishing the connection.

You may find this curious, since in the past many who have written the most profound esoteric works have claimed that they were innocently minding their own business when a master teacher came to them, perhaps in the darkness of night, and asked them to be their scribe. They outlined the glorious task ahead of them, the quantities of books they would write and the organization they would found. I have to say in all honesty that we do not work in this fashion.

Herein lies our frustration: Many of you have read that we must not be contacted because we are too busy, too grand, too glorious, too involved in carrying out the details of the divine plan. Since I am a being who exists outside of time, how could I possibly not have enough time for you? It is true that I will not answer your personal questions as to your spiritual rank and status or whether true love and prosperity exists in your future, but without your invitation and assent, I cannot intervene in your life in any fashion, nor can any of my brethren.

Remember that this particular third-dimensional reality school has been set up as a special place where souls can work with the principle of free will under the constriction of having a personal ego and while being disconnected from the Source, or All That Is. While operating under this illusion of being a separate individual, you have had infinite freedom to make infinite mistakes for an almost infinite period of time. The general idea was that you would come to voluntarily choose to align yourself with all that is good, true, unselfish and beautiful. But the general result was that a small portion of human souls became almost endlessly trapped in this illusion of reality, becoming increasingly more selfish. Therefore, it was necessary to send a rescue mission to end the game. I would not say that this particular third-dimension planetary school was in any sense a failure, since billions of souls learned to align themselves with divine will during their visit here, and then they left. Well, a large number of you who left agreed to come back and put an end to the ceaseless misery of those souls trapped here. So we work together from the fifth and third dimensions in order to put an end to this particular cycle of learning. The problem is that it is time for you to wake up from the trance you are in and remember what you came here to do and ask us for our help.

The question often arises as to why or how such a lofty personage as myself would associate with such a lowly and humble instrument as this particular channel. I hope you will realize that I say this with some ironic humor, as I have never considered myself to be anything but a human who has had many lifetimes, made many errors and often strayed from the spiritual path in order to be where I am today, which is nowhere in particular as far as you are concerned. From my point of view I am in a reality quite unlike the one you inhabit. I am surrounded by my peers, and we unanimously hold you who are incarnate in the third dimension as the heroes, just as you might revere astronauts walking on the Moon. We consider your condition and your willingness to undertake this mission of being born on a third-dimensional planet as an act of true courage and sacrifice. You knew that there would be

dangers involved, and you knew that it would not necessarily be easy, but you chose to come here at this
time to do this. We are here in the fifth dimension
ready to support you in any and every fashion possible,
but we cannot and do not act without your permission.

We consider your illusion of the separate ego to be
the most painful and unpleasant circumstance conceivable. We do not judge you for your sense of personal
and limited identity but rather grieve and empathize
with the terrible aloneness you have willingly undertaken to experience. Telepathy is as natural and normal
to us as the air you breathe. As the planet accelerates
toward the fifth dimension, many of you will break
free from the illusion of separation and experience telepathy and interconnectedness. Many will also become conscious on the astral plane in the dreaming
state and seek to learn what is happening. Once millions of you begin to experience the astral plane as a reality, a certainty that these beautiful esoteric concepts
are not fantasies will fill the consciousness of your species and the illusion of separation will be transcended.
Many will study the wisdom teachings in an effort to
understand what they are experiencing. So it is our desire that a clear explanation of the astral plane or fourth
dimension should be in place for those seeking to understand more, allowing them to remember who they
are and why they came here.

As these frequencies are stepping up, we desire to
work with greater numbers of channels as a means of
confirming the truth of what is being stated. Many of
these channels will be unknown to each other and unfamiliar with each others' work. We do not wish you to
hold any of them in any special awe, but rather to realize that this ability to make inner contact will eventu-

ally become available to the entire race. This is the direction in which you are all moving. The process of developing telepathy will begin between people who are in love or strongly attracted to each other and grow exponentially from there. The tendency to fall in love is a powerful resource in the process of breaking through the veil of illusion.

13

Some Thoughts on Love, Sex and Relationships

I would like to express some thoughts on a topic that is not discussed much in channeled teachings. It is that of love, sexuality and relationships. I am presenting this information within the framework of current discussions on the stepped-up energies being pulsed through the etheric grid of the planet.

I am lumping together love, sex and relationships in the title of this essay. Of course, each of these elements can exist independently, but for the purposes of this discussion, I wish to interrelate them.

For those of us who exist in the fifth dimension, the concept of two individuals having a loving relationship within the confinement of two separate human egos seems almost impossible at best. It often seems to be an attempt to escape the terrible sense of aloneness that arises from having a human ego. To make this situation clear by contrast, I would have to describe our state, which is that of having a distinct personality and identity, yet an all-pervasive knowingness that we, the many, are all emanations from the One and that there really is only One, combined with a telepathic flowing between our consciousnesses so that we never need be alone unless we wish to be. If I focus my consciousness on a specific entity in the fifth dimension, we are in immediate mental contact, and on this level there is never any misunderstanding, harshness or lack of love.

For you who are incarnate in the third dimension and limited in consciousness to a physical body, the task of maintaining a relationship seems insurmountable. You must depend on such qualities as good verbal communication, trust, boldness, courage and fidelity, and you must overcome and work with your envies and jealousies. This is part of an entire package specific to the third dimension, which is heavily geared toward procreation and sexuality as a means of bringing new lives into the world, and toward the family unit as a means of protecting these little ones physically, emotionally and financially. In your heavily consumer-oriented economies, love and sex are also used as marketing methods to sell consumer goods. Young adults are faced with the task of finding a partner and setting up a family unit. This is natural at this level of reality, as well as the result of hormones that begin to secrete during the teenage years.

The chakra system that exists on the higher dimensions ties into the glands that produce hormones. So at different stages of the human life cycle, various chakras kick in, activating associated glands. From roughly the age of fourteen or fifteen years, the sex and growth hormones are activated. This is the time when the second-chakra energy is activated and adolescents become seriously focused on relationships.

In the third dimension, procreation, childbirth, setting up families, falling in love and sexuality all come together as a package. So what has also evolved in the third dimension is that those souls who wished to focus on their spiritual development rather than on parenting (such as monks and nuns of all denominations) would embark on a path of celibacy, which implies that sexuality is not spiritual or has no place in the spiritual life. Nothing could in actuality be further from the truth, and I will, of course, elaborate on this further.

It is more accurate to say that in the third-dimensional reality, during thousands of years in which there was no efficient and easy birth control, it was necessary for some of the population to choose the path of celibacy. In thousands of years of recent history, the general life span also tended to be rather short, so that not many people made it past the child-bearing years. My point is that conditions were not very suitable for two people who loved each other to explore sexuality as a tool for spiritual growth in its own right, without producing children (although the tantric path does just that).

So consider sexuality from the esoteric perspective and in terms of energies. All the forms of your third-dimensional reality are built of infinitely small parcels of energy that you call atoms. Atoms are composed of subatomic particles, electrons and a nucleus. The nucleus is composed of a positively charged, magnetic proton or cluster of protons, and a neutral neutron or neutrons. The electrons that orbit the nucleus are negatively charged. When a nucleus has electrons orbiting it that match its atomic weight, the atom is neutral.

However, the nature of the atom is always a balance between positive and negative subatomic particles, which are the components of electricity. So let us give this some thought, a bit of deep reflection. When you perform a chemical reaction that releases negative electrons and positive protons in streams, you have electricity that can be harnessed and used for some purpose. When you have these same electrons and protons locked into a whirling dance around each other, you have the building blocks of manifest reality. Think of it this way: All the forms you see around you are formed from a particular type of electricity. It is not the type of free-flowing electricity you are familiar with that powers your homes; it is a fixed electricity that forms solids, liquids, gases and therefore all the forms of creation.

It is possible to view all this reality as an interchange between positively and negatively charged energy parcels. Or we might categorize these subatomic particles as feminine and masculine, or perhaps equate the positive proton charge with the feminine principle and the negative electron charge with the masculine principle. Why not the other way around?, you might wonder. For the purpose of this discussion we will associate protons with feminine energy and electrons with masculine energy. So the basic bond that holds electrons in orbit around an atomic nucleus is an attractive force, an electrical force, and when this force is applied to immense objects, such as stars or planets, it is called gravity. But when this term is applied to humans, it is called love. The definition of gravity is something like "an attractive force that draws bodies with density and mass toward each other," is it not? So if we suppose that the attractive force that binds atoms together is love, it becomes clear that love is the basis of all manifest reality.

However, the bonds that bind many atoms to form the molecules of solids and liquids function a little differently, and this is another topic. The basic relationship between the subatomic particles of the simplest atom, the hydrogen atom, might be considered a sort of marriage. I am trying to impart some sense of the inherent structure and order of the universe, which exists at every level and which repeats, as Hermes Trismegistus wrote, "As above, so below." There are numerical and electrical orders to everything, based on a simple pattern that repeats itself through every level of existence as well as on the inner planes.

So one might come to conceptualize males as being mainly, although not totally, negatively charged and females as being mainly, but not totally, positively charged. When a relationship is formed between a male and a female, an electrical circuit is created, which culminates in sexual activity. During sexual activity a veritable vortex of electricities is created on the inner planes, and pure energy from the highest god levels flows down from the inner planes through the female and back up through the male. This circuit culminates in sexual activity on the physical level, but it does not necessarily need to. A circuit can be created that terminates in the fourth-dimensional emotional level or the fifth-dimensional mental level. Sometimes it is not necessary for two individuals to form a sexual relationship; sometimes there is a chemistry present that can create art, literature or music. The electrical energies then stop short of the physical plane and sexuality, finding expression on the higher planes or dimensions.

To understand this flowing of electricities through

the inner planes, it is necessary to examine the energy flows that circulate through the primary seven chakras situated along the spine but located in the etheric body and on the fourth and fifth dimensions.

Depending on what system you have studied, you may already know that the base chakra is associated with the third-dimensional physical reality, the physical body, aggression, courage, sexuality and the color red. The second chakra is associated with the emotions, the astral plane, vitality, the digestive system and the color orange. The third chakra, the solar plexus, is associated with the lower mental plane, the ego, intellectual ability and the color yellow. And the fourth chakra is the heart chakra — balance, healing, the causal plane, Christ consciousness and the color green as well as other colors.

The kundalini fire is dormant at the base of the spine, and throughout the course of a lifetime it slowly ascends and stabilizes at the chakra where the consciousness has attained control. For most of humanity this is the second or third chakra.

Of course, this information is not new, and many of you are probably familiar with current information about the chakras.

I would like to add to this a brief description of how individuals form energy bonds between each other that take the form of strands of energies, or rays, that connect them through the chakras. In the ideal marriage two people would be seen to have a rainbow arc of light between them from the lowest chakra to the highest. It is virtually impossible for two people to perform the sexual act without some chakras becoming tied together in an energy bond, although many people are bound together on some level without engaging in the sexual act. You realize that a person who was a prostitute in one lifetime has formed ties to many individuals who may have unsavory natures, and that former prostitute will attract these same people again in future incarnations. There is a two-way flow of energy from one to another through these energy bonds, and sometimes these bonds are so enduring that they tie individuals together life after life. This explains the phenomenon of feeling strong emotions toward a virtual stranger at the first meeting.

Now I would like to add further information about the nature of these energy bonds for you to reflect on, especially in regard to your life experiences. Energy bonds take the form of cords of various colors that attach two people through their chakras. The energy bonds might be a beautiful rose-pink, signifying higher romantic love, or a more golden pink, signifying spiritual love. Tones of gold, silver, rose-pink, green, blue, indigo and violet are expressions of higher emotions that bind people. (Some of the highest emotions are not energies of the astral plane but of much higher levels.) Then there are murky colors such as muddy red, dark green and black, which are expressions of negative emotions such as cruel lust, jealousy, envy and malice. These bonds may go from the third chakra of one person to the first or second of another, or from the fourth to the fourth, depending on what level of consciousness these bonds arise. Sometimes these negative energy bonds drain energy from one to another or exert control over another. It is possible to mentally remove these negative energy cords by visualizing them and pulling them out, as in unplugging an electrical cord from a socket.

These energies I describe are a particular type of

electricity on the fourth dimension. They are streams of free-flowing negatively and positively charged sub-atomic particles that move a lot faster than third-dimensional electricity and with a different voltage. So you might conceptualize these bonds as streams of current that run between two people.

If everyone in incarnation had beautiful energy fields of pale, ethereal-colored vortexes, it would be wonderful, but because many individuals have dark, muddy, murky colors in their chakras, it is possible through the sexual act to open oneself up to either a degrading influence or an elevating influence. It depends on the strength of the individual's will and the degree of self-discipline. So it is possible for a strongly spiritually inclined individual to raise the level of consciousness of his or her partner through relationship and sexuality. It is also possible for a depraved individual to have a very degrading influence on a suggestible partner. This is purely on a level of highly charged electrical energy fields and has nothing to do with beliefs or opinions.

Have you ever seen someone who seemed to have a very pleasant, kindly, warm personality degenerate into the very opposite while being heavily under the influence of a particular love interest? What is at work here is that this individual does not have a strong will and is therefore highly suggestible to the energies emitted through the chakras of his or her partner. The reverse may also occur where an unpleasant person may change while in love with a particular person and become very different. So clearly it is important for the spiritually inclined person to find a partner of good character so that they can work together to raise each other's energies.

When the heart chakra becomes activated through a romantic involvement and the individual experiences love of one individual, it is then possible for the individual to experience a greater love that encompasses all of humanity in certain instances. Progress along the spiritual path over many lifetimes has always been spurred along by acts of sacrifice and devotion, performed for the love of one individual but expanding into a greater love.

Finally, I wish to give some consideration to the nature of the kundalini fire, which exists on the inner planes and in every human in incarnation. It is a fiery, electrical energy on the inner planes, a constant stream of higher-frequency electrons that travel through space at a faster rate than those of the physical plane. The central nervous system of the human body functions through electrochemical impulses, so it should not be a surprise to learn that the ancient Hindu concept of the kundalini is an electrical force that moves up the spinal cord to the brain, but on the inner planes. Stimulating the base chakra stimulates this energy, and it rises up the spinal cord to the level where consciousness is focused and stabilized. For instance, when two individuals engage in sexual activity and one has a much higher level of consciousness than the other, the kundalini energy might be focused at the fifth chakra. This union starts to draw the consciousness of the partner to a higher level. However, hopefully the effect of a relationship based on love and sexuality will at least raise the energies to the heart-chakra level and open the heart chakra in both individuals. In this way two lovers attain the fourth level of initiation, that of the Christ consciousness. This is the ideal and the hope for humanity.

Many of you might be wondering why, if the simple process of falling in love and entering a healthy relationship raises the consciousness of both pairs to a Christ level, this does not seem to be the case in your *real* world. How many partners do you know who display a higher consciousness or a Christ-like love of humanity? Well, I would say that the majority of couples rarely activate (mutually) the heart chakra and create a bond at that level. More often, the bonds of sexual attraction to a physical type are formed at the base chakra. The sensation of falling in love originates at the second chakra, and the third chakra binds individuals who are drawn together for ego reasons. Such people pick up members of the opposite sex as trophies and exhibit them for their appearance or some other reason.

Real love is developed over time, and sometimes it is developed over many lifetimes. So the flowering of the heart chakra is not the automatic result of forming a romantic relationship but the desired goal. It was the fire that fueled the troubadours who made courtly love the basis of the Christian tradition of love, whereas in other cultures of the time, marriages were based on status and convenience and were traditionally arranged by the parents. I am aware that Christian ideals of love predated the troubadours, but it is out of the impulse of that era that Western culture has its romantic ideals of today.

The frequencies of the planet are accelerating toward a higher dimension, and this is going to have some impact on all aspects of life in your third-dimensional reality, including relationships. Of interest to us on the inner planes is that growing numbers of people, especially young people, are interested in the concept of soulmates and utilize methods published in popular books for drawing their soulmate to them. The contact is made initially on the astral plane, and people are drawn together through this magnetic bond. In fact, one might say that it was never broken. There are several categories of soulmates, and on the highest dimensional levels, monad or divine sparks are like binary stars — one positively charged, one negatively charged — that whirl around each other in ecstasy. However, on the more tangible levels of reality, the soul journeying through incarnation travels with a cluster of souls who change their roles and relationships from life to life, so it is possible to have several potential mates available from the family constellation who might serve as life partners.

As the soul journeys through many lives and interacts with the same family of souls, the ties of love that bind are formed, and the family group is drawn together in subsequent lifetimes, not necessarily to work through karma, but simply drawn together by the power of love. Sometimes members of the family are not in incarnation and serve as guides. Souls choose before they are born to meet at some particular location in time and space. They also time their incarnation so that they are within a compatible age range. Changes in plans and other decisions are made on the inner planes while in the sleep state.

So imagine the situation as a virtual reality game. The real you exists in a cosmic game room with many other players, and you are playing this third-dimensional reality game with the intention of increasing your level of light. That is the ultimate goal. You set up the conditions of your game before you were born, based on the karmic score of previous games and what you are entitled to. You know what traits you need to overcome and what traits you need to acquire in order to increase your light. Right now you are part of a large team game, and you are working in cooperation with a lot of other players. There is a small family group of players whom you know very well, and you have entered the game as a team many, many times. Part of the game is to team up in pairs and work on an incarnation together. Whenever you go to sleep, it is as if you have turned off the game and taken off your virtual reality suit. You are back in the cosmic game room discussing the game or doing other things.

So as the energies are being accelerated, it is as if the game and the rules are changing. People within relationships will find that they are more telepathic with each other and more blended. The process of trying to maintain a relationship will become a little easier with better communication, and this will become especially true for lightworkers and those who consciously meditate on a daily basis. People will not need to demand of each other, "Do you love me?" because they will feel the love as an emanation of warmth coming from the beloved.

14

Karma, Reincarnation and Morality

One of the cornerstone teachings of the Hindu, Buddhist, theosophical and wiccan religions is that of reincarnation and karma, though these concepts are often poorly understood or open to abuse. However, they cannot be considered irrational notions, since most of humanity believes in them and has done so from the most ancient of times.

Many misunderstand reincarnation to mean the transmigration of souls, which is the false belief that human souls may come back as some lower form such as an animal or reptile. This, of course, would not serve the divine plan of spiritual evolution very well. Some argue that there are now more souls on the planet than have ever been here before in the entirety of human history, but in fact, human history has existed for a much longer time and with greater numbers of individuals than you could imagine.

Many books have been written on the subject of karma and reincarnation, so there is not a great deal to add on this theme. But there are approaches to understanding these concepts that can accelerate your spiritual development and other approaches that can hold you back.

In India the belief in reincarnation and karma has been used to maintain the status quo and keep the lower classes in place. The lower classes have been told that if they work out their karma, they might be born into a wealthier caste in a future life. This is a perfect example of how an enlightened teaching may become perverted to suit the needs of those who do not wish to trouble themselves with feelings of guilt or compassion. In similar fashion, many New Age people use the concept of karma to fuel undesirable feelings, traits and emotions. For instance, some believe that victims *deserve* their experiences. They feel that the bad karma comes from having abused others in past lives, or that poverty is due to bad karma. The simple truth is, you do not know what karmic situation causes another to suffer — or even whether it is karma at all.

When properly understood, the belief in reincarnation and karma should give an individual a sense that the universe is just, eliminate undesirable emotions (envy, jealousy and revenge) and minimize fear. You are eternal. You change form, but the conscious awareness that is you does not change or die. It gains in experience and knowledge, but it does not die. You do not reincarnate as soon as you die; you spend long periods of time on the inner planes, which are higher-frequency dimensions that interpenetrate this universe.

The only means by which you can raise your consciousness, increase the level of light energy you transmit and raise the atomic frequency of your atoms is by developing your sense of compassion and universal love. Any thought process that encourages you to be judgmental or cruel lowers your frequency level.

There is a tremendous difference in the thought processes typical to the East and West, especially in the area of religion and spirituality. Western religious thought tends to place a very heavy focus on sin and punishment and on sexuality as sinful. This has not created a society without sin, however.

From the perspective of the East, there is no personalized male god who pries into the sex life of the individual. Hinduism has its pantheons, Buddhism has the Buddha, Taoism has the Void, but sexuality is not considered to be a cause of guilt and shame to the degree that this unnatural schism has occurred in the West. In Western thinking a spiritual person is a sexless person who does good deeds. Carnality and spirituality are at opposite ends of the spectrum — the flesh and the spirit — in the West.

From the Eastern perspective this schism between spirit and flesh appears to be psychologically unhealthy, and certainly, from my vantage point, I can see that it is. Westerners are horrified if some holy man of the East has an affair. From the Eastern viewpoint this is not surprising or shocking, if the individual is acting from his highest truth and deepest feelings. The path to enlightenment demands a certain degree of authenticity. What would horrify the Eastern mentality is if this holy man exploited in a ruthless fashion the person he had an affair with.

All systems, whether Eastern or Western, propose that the person who does wrong, however wrong is defined, will suffer for it at some future time. But this is not the essence of the meaning of karma. Karma is a concept that all actions have inevitable consequences, and before acting spontaneously, one should consider the possible outcomes of a specific act.

From the esoteric standpoint, every action is preceded by a thought or an intent, which crystallizes in action and is reflected in the personal aura of the individual, visible in the fourth dimension. If the aura is full of harmful emotions that will precipitate acts of hostility toward others, the individual has set up a personal magnetic energy field that will attract energies and matter of *the exact same kind*. As we move toward the fourth dimension, this process will speed up. Then we will begin to see instant karma. Also, the process of magnetic attraction is facilitated by the devas who work with karma, and these are very specific devas.

So you have started out on the spiritual path as a beginner. Immediately all sorts of things start to go wrong in your life, and your New Age friends tell you that you are taking on many lifetimes of unresolved karma that has been saved up especially for you, just waiting for the point where your consciousness is ready for it. Well, this is not quite what happens. When things become difficult, it is because the beginner on the path is being tested to see how well he or she can embody the consciousness that this novice has been trying to attain through study, meditation and contemplation. But suffering is not a requirement of spirituality. That would serve no purpose other than to drive the beginner off the spiritual path.

The simple answer to all the confusion about karma and whether one can invoke the laws of grace, is that karma exists to teach the individual how he or she has made others feel, what others have had to suffer. If the individual can develop a better sense of empathy, compassion, humility, caring and so on, there is no need for karma that will make the individual more sensitive. Only a very insensitive, callous, selfish individual would benefit from getting many lifetimes of karma deposited on them suddenly, and if that person were just beginning to open up to a higher reality, nothing would be gained by choosing this time to start paying off karmic debts.

As it is, many of you who have learned that you are here to pay off many lifetimes of karmic debts and that you are chained to many lifetimes on Earth — *you are not.* You chose to come here; you came with a purpose. You are not tied here, you are free to leave. You are here out of love for this planet.

Often karma does not refer so much to themes of punishment, but rather changing from one kind of experience to another to balance out one's experience. If someone has been very rich and powerful, he may need to experience being downtrodden and oppressed. The soul that has memories of what it feels like to feel powerful needs to have an additional databank of the opposite information. If a woman has been a nun in one life, she may feel compelled to be a prostitute in the next. Her soul has memories of a lifetime when sexuality was avoided and feels a need to learn more by focusing on sexuality more than is normal. This is the reason the Buddha always advocated moderation in all activities. Any extreme position will require balancing. Any extreme lifestyle will create a lifetime of its opposite, and often some form of suffering is involved.

So if you examine your present life, whatever it is, it may be some sort of opposite to some other life you had in the past. The higher self always seeks to gather data and information from incarnations that show both sides of the coin. So when you take the higher initiations that lead to mastery, you will remember all of your thousands of incarnations. This will be a very difficult and upsetting experience, in a sense, because it is somewhat like watching a thousand dramatic movies in which you are the star. You are like an incredible actor who has played every human part conceivable. There will be tremendously sad love stories and epic dramas of wealth, power and status, not to mention all the lives in which you were a priest or priestess of some exotic religion. Your higher self is very much like an actor that wishes to try a wide variety of roles without become stuck in one type. There is constant change.

So you see, if in one life the higher self chose to take the role of a psychopathic killer in order to understand what such a being would be like, then another life will embody the opposite for balance, whatever the opposite might be — perhaps a police detective who specializes in homicide. The soul does not necessarily need to be the victim of a vicious killer in order to balance that experience.

As you progress along the path, fragmentary memories may surface in dreams. Usually these dreams will be linked to someone you are involved with in some way and will give insights into the emotional ties that bind you together.

15

Time and Probability

Ideas from the field of quantum physics abound these days and have had a profound influence on New Age writers. But this is not to say that because they are theories from a scientific field, they are inherently true. One pervasive notion from quantum theory is that at any given crossroads or choice, both possibilities exist and split off to form a parallel universe, and there may be an infinite number of parallel Earths with various outcomes and histories. Appealing as this idea is, it would actually serve little purpose in the scheme of the Creator's plan of spiritual evolution. The truth is, there are infinite possible futures in the realm of the fourth dimension, most of which never come into expression in the third dimension. There is *only one* third-dimensional reality.

One might also conceive of time as being set from beginning to end, much like a reel of film is set. As the film moves across the light that projects it onto a screen, the illusion of motion through time is created. Some have suggested that all the events of history are set, and consciousness is analogous to the light of the projector. As third-dimensional reality moves across consciousness, the illusion of moving through time is created. While these are fascinating, mind-expanding concepts to play with, the truth is that the future in the third dimension is open, not set or known. What does exist is an infinite number of astral possibilities created by the collective consciousness of humanity, which exists at higher and lower levels and very often is what psychics see when they think they are getting a vision of the future. So there are levels of possibility where the future holds massive destruction, and there are possibilities of the future where many of the most serious problems facing humanity are solved. All of you are the crucial and deciding factors.

So we might use a metaphor of time that is more like the process of making a movie. In the middle of the movie, we have some footage and are following a screenplay, an idea. However, after rehearsing and thinking about the screenplay, we might decide that it doesn't really work, so we might change or modify it. Unexpected things might happen, and we might have to cancel some days of shooting or even replace an actor. We have a general idea of where things are going, but we haven't shot the remaining portion of the film. In other words, humanity rehearses events of the future in the dream state, and *you* decide whether this is the direction in which you wish to go.

You might be wondering about the possibility of entities traveling through time.

Perhaps you have read somewhere that this is possible and that humans are being sent into the future or the past, or that this was done in the past even at the time of Atlantis and so on. But what is actually happening is that beings are moving up in frequency into the fourth dimension, going into some astral past or future, then returning to their starting point in the third dimension.

I cannot emphasize enough that even as I am a master who exists outside time (which means that I am not in synchronization with your time frame), I am not entirely outside time and clearly viewing everything from beginning to end. I can clearly see *some* of the probabilities that lie in your future, but I cannot tell how it will all work out. You might try to picture time and the dimensions in terms of a large wheel with spokes and a hub. At the outer rim of the wheel is time and at the center there is no time, but all time can be seen from all directions. Well, where I am is slightly up one of the spokes!

What I do know is that we have planned for these coming times like a military operation. First we sent a few scouts, then we sent an intelligence group. Following that we sent a vanguard, an advance guard and a second wave. As time progresses we are sending more and more lightworkers to act as anchors for the light on the planet. Not only do we have the troops in place, but we have a schedule of the cosmic energies we are releasing through the etheric web of the planet, which will accelerate the evolution of the planet and all life forms on it.

Thus I know what we accomplished and what we have planned as well as what we plan to do. I also know that the solar system is rushing through space, not to enter a physical photon belt in space so much as to reach coordinates that will put the planet in alignment with certain cosmic forces coming through the zodiac. These forces will inevitably have specific effects on humanity. They are, of course, the influences of Aquarius, and it is generally known that the qualities associated with this golden age are those of brotherhood, equality and high technology. So we can anticipate an era of advanced technology combined with a leveling of humanity where all are considered equal. We have already seen much of this in the past hundred years. These have been turbulent times (though this is not a requirement), and as the energy increases, more turbulence can be expected.

So we on the inner planes and you who chose to be born on Earth at this time to inaugurate a change have been working together to prevent a future filled with catastrophes. You may have heard from some channels that Gaia needs to purify herself, so she is causing bad weather conditions all over the planet. The truth is, Gaia is working with the elementals, attempting to stabilize the conditions of the planet.

On this theme of stabilizing the planet, I would like to emphasize that this is what the lightworkers are here to do. All of you have the power to work with the elementals who in turn work with the weather, keeping Earth and weather patterns stable in your area. From the viewpoint of the great being who is the consciousness of the planet, an endless series of weather catastrophes such as earthquakes, hurricanes, tornadoes, forest fires and massive floods are experienced as symptoms of a serious illness, and the loss of human lives is analogous to a human's having a stroke or other serious physical condition. So no, Earth is not purifying the planet at this time. As a lightworker, you can engage in brief daily meditations in which you mentally ask the weather beings for stable weather in your area. In the same fashion you can attempt to anchor peace, calm and prosperity.

At the time this is being written, we are clearly moving into what appear to be difficult and dangerous times. The world economy is unstable, terrorist activity is escalating and in a short time the looming threat of a computer crisis could impact the entire planet. So you, the lightworkers, have stationed yourselves here to hold the image of a positive future for humanity and make your own energies so harmonious that the angelic kingdoms will work with you. See yourselves as anchor points in a chain of beings that extends higher and higher into brighter and brighter light. Ask mentally to join with them. Higher beings will never violate free will, so this translates to: If you need their help, you must ask for it.

Some of you may have noticed that the quality of teaching these days is very different from the earlier teachings. Rather than emphasizing selflessness and planetary service, New Age books are largely how-to books, telling individuals how to increase their prosperity and general conditions. They seem to have a self-centered focus, one might think. Generally, the conditions that might make an individual uncomfortable enough to search for new answers to the meaning of life (answers different from the traditional religion the individual was raised in, such as lack of love and money and a general sense of confusion about life) are conditions and factors built into the life plan by the soul as a means to provide a time for that individual to wake up and remember why he or she is here. The very acts involved in raising the level of light energy within oneself tie in with the work of serving the planet, and once a person starts to become a conscious, meditating lightworker, he or she joins a great force of planetary lightworkers and higher beings.

The ultimate important point to make about the nature of time and the future is that you are creating it moment by moment through the power of your collective thoughts and emotions. If you hold negative ideas about the future, you are shaping a negative future, perhaps not for all of humanity, but locally where you are. Also, as the energies of the planet are being consciously accelerated, the thoughts you hold have more power.

As we reach and pass this turn of the millennium, there are many sources promoting the concept of negative outcomes. This is intentional, because mass thoughts of fear, panic and terror can be harnessed by the counterforces and used to further their ends. You see this every day. The newspapers, movies, TV shows and music focus on violence, destruction and horrible futures. *Do not participate in this type of thinking.* Take time to imagine a positive future for yourself, your friends, your family and the planet.

16

Dealing with Daily Life

My partner in this project has asked me to offer some insight into how one might deal with daily life and difficult people and circumstances. Certainly, spiritual self-help books abound with suggestions of how to deal with difficult people. They include such techniques as mentally visualizing sitting down with them, talking with them, explaining one's own position and resolving situations with others through the use of inner work, such as holding them in love and light. These suggestions will be effective in a certain number of cases where there is some misunderstanding.

At this time there is a force of accumulated negativity on this planet that seeks to hold back progress. It is somewhat like a battle for the destiny of the planet. There are many individuals who have made themselves the unwitting tools of planetary evil. What I mean by this is that there are many people who have not consciously aligned themselves with the principles of goodness and truth and who are mainly bent on getting whatever they want for themselves with no regard for the cost to others. These people do not feel accountable for their actions. By contrast, in the Middle Ages in Europe, people lived very simple lives without technology. They lived in huts, grew their own food, tended animals and fashioned their tools and clothing from simple materials. Practically everyone believed in heaven and hell, felt accountable for their actions to each other and tried to lead lives that would please the Master Jesus.

Now, I am not saying there was never any crime or ill will or that passions never got out of hand, but when they did, the individuals usually felt a great deal of guilt, fear and remorse for their acts. For most of them, the hope of attaining heaven was a reality, and they suffered through the most miserable conditions with the ever-present hope of reuniting with their loved ones.

If we contrast this to the situation today, we see that many consider the possibility of heaven a childish fantasy, designed simply as a means of social control. They say that science has proven it to be nonsense. Scientists who have searched the human body say they cannot find such a thing as a soul that might survive death. Of course, they cannot explain what consciousness is or how the brain actually works or where or how memories are stored in the brain, or why the act of observing a particle influences its behavior. Now we have a new phenomenon of the near-death experience, which is actually a death experience. Science explains this away as "some hallucinogen released by the brain during the dying process."

I mention all this because the deepest pain any person can feel is the certain belief that a loved one who has died has entirely ceased to exist. Other sources of psychological pain are a deep sense of the randomness and meaninglessness of life. The scientific materialism that prevails today seeks to dispute and disparage any evidence of survival of the spirit after death. As indications accumulate to suggest the possibility of the reality of the inner dimensions, many people live through their existence in deeper pain and despair than is necessary. Also, it is of the utmost importance to note that when an individual is immersed in grief, it is virtually impossible for the presence of the departed to make itself felt. Nevertheless, many who experience the loss of a loved one sense a presence at times or have mental conversations with the departed spirit.

On the other hand, we see in the world today a great many fanatic religious sects that function on the premise of creating an elite of individuals who will survive catastrophes and be elevated as a select group to some future heaven world. The driving force behind these religious sects is elitism and hatred for all those who do not share their particular interpretation of scripture or religious teachings.

Inclusiveness is the hallmark of these groups that are affiliated with the higher spiritual powers, and no soul is ever lost or damned. Nor does a soul lose the chance of attaining a higher level of consciousness. Within the Buddhist framework, for example, those who are not living according to a higher consciousness are doomed to be incarnated on Earth over and over again until they consciously break free of the bonds of reincarnation and find union with a higher consciousness. But no soul is ever lost.

Faced on the one hand with so many fanatical and

loctrines that do not embody the basics of a *' consciousness* (inclusiveness, compassion and love for all humanity, with the hope that all souls may find some salvation at some time) and with scientifically based atheism on the other, many individuals turn to alcohol, drugs and the philosophy of "eat, drink and be merry, for tomorrow we die." When people function at this low level of consciousness and carry around a great deal of bitterness and pain at the unfairness of life, they open the doors that make it possible for them to be used as pawns of malevolence and planetary evil.

So in a sense, mentally connecting to such people and sending them love and light is certainly a better approach than sending them thoughts of hatred and anger, which would only increase their power. If they are the type who revel in abusing their personal power and position by making others miserable, then a better approach is to ask for the assistance of the angels when dealing with them. In this case, a person would invoke the angel of justice.

As to those particular entities on the inner planes that you refer to as angels: They have been described in all cultures at all times and in various ways as the messengers of God. They also have the power to assist and save people who are in danger and have other abilities to protect and help. You may have noticed that in the past decade there has been an increase of interest in angels, and more and more people are talking and writing about them. This is another phenomenon, perhaps even a sign, that the energy of the planet is increasing, because the planet is coming closer and closer to the frequency of the angelic kingdom and they can reach you more easily and have more effect on you.

Angels respond to prayer, which is the creation of a

thought form directed to a higher power. This is perfectly tangible to them. They have been charged with acting on the reasonable prayers of incarnate humanity under certain strictures: They will not violate the free will of another or act as instruments of harm to another. However, one may ask for their protection, healing and assistance and ask them to protect loved ones. You do not need to have a crisis of any kind to invoke the presence of the angelic hosts. If you feel depressed, you can ask for the angel of joy to come to you. If you feel worried, you can ask for the presence of the angel of peace. If you have money worries, you can ask for angel of prosperity to aid you. It is all in the asking. So I suggest that you suspend disbelief and try this as an experiment, perhaps keeping a diary of the outcomes. You do not need to be a saint to make this work for you, but just an average person of goodwill who is looking for answers and striving to increase your spiritual understanding.

So let us assume that you are a person who has become tired of the limited teachings of organized religion and are leading a fairly ordinary life, dealing with friends and family and trying to maintain an occupation. What do you need to do to make your life more spiritual?

Well, I would say that a common error people make at this stage is that they search to find a spiritual group of people or some organization based on the mysteries. They look for a teacher in the area of the physical world. In some books it is actually written, "When the pupil is ready, the teacher appears," so whatever teacher they run into, they generally assume that they are progressing along the path. Well, at this period it is time to act on the inner authority from inner teachers, not ex-

ternal teachers out in the world. Any good spiritual
teacher will direct you from within. In fact, you will
know that you are on the right track if you find some
particular group that directs you inward toward your
own higher self.

What also tends to happen is that in the process of
getting involved with some particular group, the spiritual seeker becomes slowly disillusioned when it is dis-
covered that the leaders of the group have human frailties of some sort. This also tends to lend a sense
disillusionment to the teachings.

The fact is, this is not the time to be a follower of
some cult leader. Many cult groups appear in the news
after some awful disaster, which gives a certain chilling
sense that spiritual groups are dangerous, and to a large
extent they can be. It is certainly not desirable that any
of you hand over your inner authority to someone else
and act on their pronouncements. Inevitably we see
over and over again that individuals are exploited financially and sexually, or are just abused by pathological
leaders with some sort of charisma. Well, of course
there are genuine teachers out there, but their hallmark
of integrity is that they will not tell you what to do,
how to live your life or tell you that you are joining an
elite. But they *will* show you how to meditate, heal
others and find your own inner source of inspiration,
your own inner contacts.

I propose that you open up to the possibility that
there is more to reality than rationalists would have
you believe. You are not to join any group, but to study
the vast variety of metaphysical books on your own,
looking for New Age books with guided visualizations.
Now, I do not mean that you absolutely must not
come together with some New Age people in a study

or healing group, but that your focus should always remain within yourself.

You might want to make lifestyle changes, such as giving up red meat or smoking — and certainly, giving up drinking alcohol or taking illegal drugs. Perhaps you consider this latter point harsh and judgmental coming from a master, but on the inner realms we do not condone either illegal behavior or toxic behavior, and we consider alcohol and illegal drugs as slow-acting poisons to the brain. They damage the delicate receptors required in inner work. Also, it is quite possible for the use of such toxic agents to damage the delicate etheric web that protects the chakras, because there is a subtle interplay between the neurotransmitters and hormones released by glands and the chakra system. Illegal drugs imitate existing neurotransmitters in the body, but when they are used at the wrong time and stage of development, they can open various chakras out of sequence. Thus there is a possibility of opening up to psychic possession, which happens a lot more frequently than you might think.

If you think about it, you might know someone in your circle of acquaintances who has an illegal drug habit or perhaps some problem with overuse of alcohol. You may notice a generally intolerant and judgmental attitude, as if they are always looking for the very worst in others. You also likely know people like that who do not abuse substances, but often this is an indication of some minor possession by a lower entity. It is very subtle.

This phenomenon is sometimes referred to as a crack in the aura, and while this is not actually the case, this is how it appears clairvoyantly. It appears that the energy field on the inner planes is cracked, which makes it possible for entities — who are not clear about where they are, who are close to the Earth plane and who envy incarnate humans their ability to live and enjoy life — to invade the consciousness and make their victims say and do things that are harmful to their spiritual growth or to their lives in general.

I know there are popular books describing shamanistic means of attaining higher knowledge, and some include drug use, but these shamans are acting within the framework of a cultural discipline and a lifetime of taking various tests and initiations to the point where they may use these substances as aids. This is rarely true for those outside their culture.

I also know that many toxic drugs are described as "natural" because they are extracted from plants, but of course you know that this argument is very weak. Many deadly poisons can be extracted from plants. You are accustomed to thinking of the term "poison" to mean something that kills you outright, but we see it in a broader context as a substance that harms and damages you.

Perhaps you may wish to work on some of your habits that are not compatible with the spiritual life. At the same time it is tempting to try to convert or illuminate close family members. This is generally not advisable unless they show an interest in your beliefs.

Rather than wasting years bouncing around from one spiritual group to another looking for a teacher, find a time and space in your home where you can meditate for a short time daily. The goal of your meditations may vary, but generally you should attempt to open yourself to the hints and suggestions of your own higher self. You must make your mind still and tranquil like a lake that holds the bright image of the full moon at night. You are also going to consciously anchor light on the planet. You may study various books from New Age bookstores and incorporate visualizations into your daily work.

I am not suggesting that you should avoid working with others, but you should find that as you study the esoteric teachings and do your own light work, you will make your own light contacts and not be caught up in the power trips and confusion created by many sincere (or not so sincere) groups. What you may find is that more interesting coincidences begin to happen and you are led to the right people.

17

The Christ

There was a time when there was a great deal of anticipation for the return of the Christ at the end of the century. You may have noticed that very little is being written about the return of the Christ at this time. What is happening is that while an individual Christ is not reappearing, a group Christ composed of many souls who have attained the fourth initiation, the Christ initiation, is forming on the planet — the lightworkers who form the esoteric body of the Christ on the planet. These souls are anchor points for the energy of the cosmic Christ, which, in a universal principle of education, healing, love and wisdom, stands in relation to the Source or All That Is as a Son principle.

There are rumors, of course, that the Master Maitreya, who holds the office of Christ, is currently living in south London in the Asian community there and that the world has studiously avoided his invitations to be interviewed in the media. The office of

Christ is that of planetary world teacher who will create the world religion that will unite all religions into one complex whole.

However, before the Christ as world teacher can return and be publicly acknowledged, a few steps have to be taken by humanity. This is a freewill zone. It is a special freewill experiment. There are rules that must be followed. On the other hand, the cries of a suffering humanity have created a special dispensation from All That Is to end this cycle and proceed to a higher and kinder cycle.

On one hand, the Christ has never left this planet. His energy is always here, grounded in the very soil. He does not appear and announce himself because humanity has not reached a point where the planet is ready for him. Humanity has to solve the basic problems that have been created. There are problems of mass starvation, war, homelessness and torture on a world level, as well as the extinction of species and the pollution of the planet.

Preparing the way for the Christ is the consciousness of the planet herself — Terra, Gaia, Mother Earth. The concept of the Earth Mother has become a rallying call to environmentalists, protectionists and a whole slew of groups to unite and plan for the future in a positive way. This work is being undertaken under the direction of the planetary consciousness, Gaia, since she has direct access to the unconscious minds of all humanity in a fashion that other beings, even masters, do not. Her consciousness has only become active, as if she has awakened from a slumber, within the past fifteen years or so, and it has been a slow and gradual process. She works most effectively with the young, as they are more focused on the future than the elderly.

So the dreaming (yet awake) consciousness of Gaia is working with the unconscious minds of humanity and the elementals and devas to solve the problems of humanity and prepare the way for the coming of the Christ. But before this can happen, there needs to be a sufficient body of people who embody Christ consciousness, the energy of the Christ, which means that they have attained the fourth initiation and have an activated heart chakra. This is not so difficult, however, since millions of fourth-degree initiates chose to incarnate at the end of the war. But many have fallen under the spell of the material world and have forgotten what they came here to do. Many became completely confused once they incarnated.

For instance, there was John Lennon, who was a high-degree initiate on the ray of Harmony through Conflict, who came to help millions of his peers wake up and gain their direction through music. This was his mission. Of course, he did not know that he was a high initiate with a mission, because if he had remembered this properly, he might have had a clearer sense of his path. He is one of millions of souls who came in with a plan and a purpose and became confused and lost while trying to function on the Earth plane. At a soul level he made a decision to end his mission because he was in danger of falling back to a lower level of consciousness. "Ah, but Master," you say, "he was shot by a madman." Remember that he has simply returned to the heart of his ashram, to his master on the inner planes, to review that incarnation. He communicates as best he can with his loved ones when they sleep.

I anticipate some skepticism, especially from older Theosophist readers. John Lennon is not your concept of a high initiate? Consider his short life and the impact he had on the young people of his day. Consider that he felt compelled to make himself look like a latter-day Jesus and that he taught love and peace through music. His mission was to end war — through music. His beingness spoke compellingly to young people. His message *reached* people.

You might say that he was testing the waters for other highly evolved souls. Clearly, humanity is not ready for the Christ, because very likely some fanatical psychotic Christian would shoot him for not matching that individual's concept of what a Christ should be. That really is a problem. I am not suggesting that John Lennon was the only highly evolved soul to enter into Earth life with a mission or that all such beings have a high visibility or that he was more special than other members of the Beatles. He was someone quite loving, wise and evolved who took up the position of a world teacher and died an untimely death. If anyone is shot who proclaims that we should all love each other, live in peace without war, treat each other as equals and hold dreams of a future where everyone lives in peace, equality and brotherhood (Aquarian ideals), then you might imagine that the Christ is in no hurry to make himself public! (He cannot actually be harmed physically, you understand, but humanity must attain a collective level of higher consciousness before he returns.)

Also, while I am being radical, I might have you consider what political party the Christ would be affiliated with, from what you already know of the teachings of the Master Jesus. (Now, there are some of you who are confused by the correlation of the masters Jesus and Christ, and I would remind you that everything the Master Jesus said in his ministry was an expression of the love and wisdom of the Christ force that overlighted him.)

What did the Master teach? People don't seem to know or remember. Did he teach that good Christians should be self-righteous, judgmental, unforgiving, moralizing hypocrites? No, he taught that people should seek the kingdom of heaven within themselves, just as I am telling you that you must look inside yourselves in your meditations. He also told people that they should love God, themselves and each other and love goodness. He said that the oppressed, the poor and the meek would inherit the Earth. He told his followers not to judge others. My point is, many of those who most vocally claim to be his followers and who claim to uphold standards of morality and Christianity would probably be standing in line to shoot him if he did not meet their particular standards! Perhaps he might appear to be born into a family on welfare in these times, or return as a black or gay man or as a woman!

So the Christ works behind the scenes, waiting for the right time — the time when the energy of the planet is sufficiently high and there are enough people of the right consciousness doing the right things — to return to the world. And this might not be anytime soon. In a sense, many souls have come in on a Christ mission and made a sudden exit from the world stage. They have talked of peace, equality and compassion for the sick and they have sought to establish a pattern of goodness. They have seeded the planet with contemporary Christ patterns. (Martin Luther King, John Lennon, Princess Diana and others might all be said to be single cells that form part of the body of the planetary Christ.)

Perhaps because we who are the spiritual government of this planet do not interfere with the physical government of the planet, it is tempting to imagine that humanity and human government is all there is. However, once you pass over to our side, or die, you discover that we have always been here. We have always tried to leave guideposts, teachings and lights in the darkness to prepare you for what is to come. What is to come after this life is a purification process of traveling through many dimensions of consciousness. There are no real hells, and there is no location where the consciousness is doomed to stay for eternity. However, the surest way to grow and make progress is simply to deal with the daily hassles and problems of being human.

Although we may not be certain as to how the future will unfold, a great army of spiritual beings is amassing on this planet in the fifth dimension to assist the spiritual government and consciousness of the planet with this major transition. Some call this planetary ascension. The speed of the change will depend to a great extent on the collective consciousness of humanity, and we will pace ourselves to match this.

As the planet is suffused with the light of the Christ, it will accelerate on the path of return and many spiritual seekers will find that they are contacting their higher selves and guides, thus acting as anchor points for the light energies of the Christ. As this army of lightworkers anchors the energies of the Christ light, the physical area around them will be an area of stable energies that the planetary being, Gaia, and the devas can use to maintain stable weather conditions and clear away negativity. The more anchors there are, the more energy will be released.

Some of this energy will initially have some disturbing effects as unconscious elements of human consciousness are being brought to the surface. This may take the form of increased interpersonal conflict and general turbulence. As the energies increase, more and more people will experience the miraculous in their lives. The planet will seem to be the same, but positive changes will be continuously taking place.

You won't wake up one morning to find that the world has completely changed or that the new age has begun. It will be a slowly developing process in which a higher consciousness of greater kindness, more awareness of spiritual truths and better ways to live life will slowly envelop the most ordinary people. More groups will organize to demand an end to the dark ways of the past. It will be remarkable, as the energies step up, to see the increasing ability of the race to experience telepathy and astral experiences and learn the ancient wisdom tradition from temples of learning located on the inner planes.

Synopsis of The Diamond Light

The Diamond Light presents wisdom teachings from the discarnate Master Djwhal Khul that have been telepathically channeled by a most ordinary person, a woman struggling to raise two teenagers as a single parent, living in poverty in the USA to demonstrate that higher spiritual beings are the most interested in those souls who need them and their help the most. The channel is not a lecturer, teacher, author or presenter of workshops, but an ordinary woman struggling with life and seeking answers to her questions about the nature of reality.

The Master's name first became known through the telepathic channelings of Alice A. Bailey, who produced seventeen thick volumes of theosophical treatises during the period between two world wars. *The Diamond Light* is intended to stand by contrast as a very short, concise, simple work that expounds the same theosophical teachings in modern terms for the general reader. Djwhal Khul deliberately blends concepts presented in the Seth material channeled by Jane Roberts with the theosophical cosmology and ties in other contemporary channeled materials to explain and illustrate that this is a special time in Earth history and that the future of the planet depends on the collective positive expectations of humanity, which will collectively form the future outcomes by the power of its collective imaginings.

The Diamond Light touches on a number of esoteric topics and interrelated themes, such as the masters, the

es or dimensions, cosmic rays, the devic and
ngdoms, the initiations and the ascension
hese concepts are tied to exercises and prac-
d to everyday living with annoying coworkers, problems with money and coping with reality. This
book is aimed at the ordinary person struggling with
life and its challenges, who senses some truth higher
than that found in traditional religions.

The Master teaches that there was once a compre-
hensive religion that combined principles of physics
and chemistry with spiritual discipline. It was shattered
and split into fragments, the pieces of which are found
in the pagan and Judeo-Christian cultures around the
planet. The current trend toward scientific materialism
has left many human souls lost and confused as they
imagine each passing day taking them one step further
toward death and oblivion. But the Master reminds us
that this reality is an illusion created by the interaction
of subatomic particles, and that other dimensions exist
where the electrons orbit the atomic nucleus at speeds
faster than light and are therefore imperceptible to us
and all of our modern technology.

Short and easy to read, *The Diamond Light* brings a
message of optimism and hope that the challenges facing humanity in the new millennium can be met and
overcome while spiritual energies are currently flooding the planet and raising the atomic frequency to
higher levels, thereby creating changes in human
awareness. Those who are waking up to the fact that
something unusual is going on can act as anchor points
for this influx of special energy by meditating daily and
following the simple instructions presented in the
book on how to meditate effectively.

The Amethyst Light

Perhaps you are standing in a bookstore thumbing through the pages of this little book, wondering if this book contains the insights you are looking for. Perhaps you are wondering who the Ascended Master Djwhal Khul is and whether he really exists or ever did. Ultimately, it does not matter who the source is, but whether the contents are enlightening and useful to you and whether, after reading this book, you can understand more metaphysics and the significance of the present time in Earth history.

My perspective is that of one who has been a Tibetan Buddhist monk who eventually presided over a monastery. In that life I focused on meditation, contemplation, study, simple chores and training and teaching younger monks. This life culminated many others spent in the monasteries of the Orient and in more mundane activities. The contemplative life makes it possible to raise consciousness to higher levels, and it is a testing ground to see how well one has learned the principles one has studied.

The goals of my Tibetan incarnation were to attain my true Buddha nature, demonstrate my compassion for all sentient beings, break free of the bonds of reincarnation and join the Noble Ones. Thus I am writing this book as one who has attained these goals and who now dwells in what might be considered a different dimension. Or I might be referred to as a mind without a body! At the time when I transcended to a higher level, I gained insights into a greater realm of knowledge and wisdom than had been available to me as a man incarnated on Earth. So I am not writing from the perspective of a Buddhist, but from that of one of the spiritual hierarchy who guides the life on this planet.

ISBN 1-891824-41-4 $**14**.95

Topics Include -

- The Seven Rays as Fields of Endeavor
- The Evolution of a World Forum
- The Planetary Chakras and the Angelic Beings
- The World Economy as a Reflection of Human Values and Creativity
- Replacing the Word "Love" with "Kindness"
- You Came to Earth on a Mission
- Meditations
- Giving Personal Channeled or Psychic Readings
- Astrology Works through the Collective Unconscious Mind
- Reflections on the Immediate Future
- A Word on the Great Invocation
- Links to the Stars

LIGHT TECHNOLOGY PUBLISHING

Call us at
1-800-450-0985
or log on
www.lighttechnology.com

THE ANCIENT SECRET
OF THE FLOWER OF LIFE
VOLUME 1

Once, all life in the universe knew the Flower of Life as the creation pattern, the geometrical design leading us into and out of physical existence. Then from a very high state of consciousness, we fell into darkness, the secret hidden for thousands of years, encoded in the cells of all life.

Now, we are rising from the darkness and a new dawn is streaming through the windows of perception. This book is one of those windows. Drunvalo Melchizedek presents in text and graphics the Flower of Life Workshop, illuminating the mysteries of how we came to be.

Sacred geometry is the form beneath our being and points to a divine order in our reality. We can follow that order from the invisible atom to the infinite stars, finding ourselves at each step. The information here is one path, but between the lines and drawings lie the feminine gems of intuitive understanding. You may see them sparkle around some of these provocative ideas:

- Remembering our ancient past
- The secret of the Flower unfolds
- The darker side of our present/past
- The geometries of the human body
- The significance of shape and structure

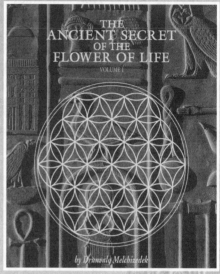

ISBN 1-891824-17-1
Soft cover, 228 p.

$25⁰⁰

Available from your favorite bookstore or:

LIGHT TECHNOLOGY PUBLISHING
P.O. Box 3540 • Flagstaff, AZ 86003
(928) 526-1345 • (800) 450-0985 • FAX (928) 714-1132
Or use our on-line bookstore:www.lighttechnology.com

SHAMANIC SECRETS for PHYSICAL MASTERY

COMING SOON

The purpose of this book is to allow you to understand the sacred nature of your own physical body and some of the magnificent gifts it offers you. When you work with your physical body in these new ways, you will discover not only its sacredness, but how it is compatible with Mother Earth, the animals, the plants, even the nearby planets, all of which you now recognize as being sacred in nature. It is important to feel the value of oneself physically before one can have any lasting physical impact on the world. The less you think of yourself physically, the less likely your physical impact on the world will be sustained by Mother Earth.

If a physical energy does not feel good about itself, it will usually be resolved; other physical or spiritual energies will dissolve it because it is unnatural. The better you feel about your physical self when you do the work in the previous book as well as this one and the one to follow, the greater and more lasting will be the benevolent effect on your life, on the lives of those around you and ultimately on your planet and universe. SOFTCOVER 600P.

$19⁹⁵ ISBN 1-891824-29-5

Chapter Titles:

- **Cellular Clearing of Traumas, Unresolved Events**
- **Cellular Memory**
- **Identifying Your Body's Fear Message**
- **The Heart Heat Exercise**
- **Learn Hand Gestures**
  - —Remove Self-Doubt
  - —Release Pain or Hate
  - —Clear the Adrenals or Kidneys
  - —Resolve Sexual Dysfunction
- **Learning the Card Technique for Clarifying Body Message**
- **Seeing Life as a Gift**
- **Relationship of the Soul to Personality**
- **The New Generation of Children**
- **The Creator and Religions**
- **Food, Love & Addictions**
- **Communication of the Heart**
- **Dreams & Their Significance**
- **The Living Prayer/Good Life**
- **Life Force and Life Purpose**
- **Physical Mastery**
- **His Life/ Mandate for His Ancestors/ Importance of Animals/ Emissaries**
- **Physical Mastery**
- **Talking to Rain/ Bear Claw Story**
- **Disentanglement**
- **Grief Culture**
- **Closing Comments**

LIFE WITH A
COSMOS CLEARANCE

Daniel M. Salter as told to Nancy Red Star

. . . IF THE GOVERNMENT DOES NOT COME FORWARD WITH THE TRUTH, THEN THE ALIENS WILL TAKE A MORE PUBLIC ROLE IN DISCLOSURE.

On May 9, 2001, the Disclosure Project hosted a major event at the National Press Club in Washington, D.C. This historic event had witness testimony from twenty to twenty-five military, intelligence, government and corporate individuals, involved with UFO projects over the last fifty years, who presented their information before a worldwide group of media correspondents.

Those of us who were military witnesses of UFO history showed **OFFICIAL GOVERNMENT DOCUMENTATION** with our detailed testimony. Our focus was and is on the facts and documents. Our purpose was and is to get the mainstream media and government officials to hear those facts and move us toward an honest congressional inquiry.

We who came forward want to **BAN WEAPONS FROM SPACE** and stop aggressively shooting down these space vehicles and their extraterrestrial occupants. We need to declassify the advanced electromagnetic propulsion systems in use by the secret government, start producing them for the world to use and thereby help save this planet.

The people who had been employed in agencies within the military and knew **THE TRUTH ABOUT UFOS** had been sworn to secrecy. Now I am finally relieved to speak the truth. We military men who hold on to this knowledge are getting old and dying, and we want the truth to come out. We will either do it ourselves or leave it for our children and wives to do.

Personally, I have told those on Capitol Hill that I am being led to do it by the aliens themselves. They have convinced me that it is time. They have been waiting on the government, and if the government does not come forward with the truth, then the aliens will take a more public role in disclosure.

—Daniel M. Salter ISBN 1-891824-37-6 $19.95

Highlights Include

- The Kalahari Retrievals
- Weaponizing Space
- From Void to Mass: Wave Particlization
- Vienna and the Black Sun
- Germany's Advanced Technologies Prior to WWII
- The Brotherhood Lodges
- Secret Deep Underground Military Bases and Advanced Earth Craft
- Star Wars
- Russian UFO Files for Sale
- Approaching the Millennium Shift
- The Wingmakers and the Ancient Arrow Site

Agent Daniel M. Salter is a retired former counterintelligence agent for the Scientific and Technical Unit of Interplanetary Phenomena in Washington D.C.. He was a member of the Pilot Air Force, NRO (National Reconnaissance Office) and DCCCD (Development of Conscious Contact Citizenry Department) with the United States military. He was a CON-RAD courier for President Eisenhower, with a clearance far above Top Secret (Cosmos) and a member of the original Project Blue Book. His expertise was in radar and electronics, his field of investigation UFOs, Aliens and Particlization. Now seventy-five, Salter has both Comanche and French ancestry.

P.O. BOX 3540 • FLAGSTAFF • AZ 86003 PHONE: (928) 526-1345 1-800-450-0985
FAX: (928) 714-1132 1-800-393-7017 www.sedonajournal.com

HINING THE LIGHT SERIES

ZOOSH AND OTHERS THROUGH ROBERT SHAPIRO

Zoosh and Others through Robert Shapiro
(Shining the Light I-VI)

YHWH through Arthur Fanning
(Shining the Light I-IV)

HINING THE LIGHT IV
JMANITY'S GREATEST CHALLENGE

ludes information on Hale-Bopp, SSG, all updates since Volume III and material the uncreating of Hitler in 1993. ✦ Negative Sirians coming to the third nension ✦ The express bus to creatorship ✦ The poison HAARP proj- ✦ Luciferian traits and critical mass ✦ ETs in Brazil ✦ Comet brings htbeing-filled vehicle bigger than Earth ✦ Sinister secret government der control of beings from the alternate negative future

SOFTCOVER 557P. $14⁹⁵ ISBN 0-929385-93-4

HINING THE LIGHT V
JMANITY IS GOING TO MAKE IT!

ɔsh and others blast the cover off past events and hidden forces at work on this plan- ɪnd reveal opportunities for immense growth and power. This is a pivotal time as secrets and mysteries that have so long bewildered humanity are at last illuminat- by the light of truth. ✦ Revelations about Area 51 by a rocket scientist ✦ A -year-long Zeta restructuring of the past ✦ Cloning: the new ethics forum Recent UFO activity in the skies ✦ The first humans and the original dark e, our shadow ✦ Angels: guides in training (30% of humans are angels) ✦ ing manifestation powers to avert man-made disasters ✦ The angel of swell ✦ Symbiotic spacecraft engines and faster-than-light travel ✦ The true rpose of the Mayans ✦ The SSG downs military planes ✦ The SSG realizes they need cus- ners, not slaves ✦ Grid lines rising above the planet ✦ Homework for changing your past

SOFTCOVER 460P. $14⁹⁵ ISBN 1-891824-00-7

HINING THE LIGHT VI
IE END OF WHAT WAS

Don't use water for fuel, or Earth will look like Mars ✦ SSG command on't read!" on U.S. TV sets ✦ How to aid whales caught in worldwide nic radiation ✦ Cats as our teachers ✦ The arrival of the wisdom seek- s and wisdom givers ✦ Zero point and the unified field ✦ Creator flips e switch ✦ Tunnels under Phoenix and white light in New England ✦ ygen-eating meteoroids ✦ Don't let the SSG draw you into a malevolent ne line ✦ Kids will lead the movement to embrace outcasts ✦ Sand as ystal libraries ✦ Hacker, an SSG dupe, causes Titan 4 rocket explosion And more

SOFTCOVER 316P. $14⁹⁵ ISBN 1-891824-24-

THE ENCYCLOPEDIA OF THE SPIRITUAL PAT

The Encyclopedia of the Spiritual Path consists of thirteen books and an index in this ongoing series on the subject of **ascension, self-realization** and a further deepening of the ascended-master teachings.

These books collectively explore the **deepest levels** and understanding of ascension through the personal, planetary and cosmic levels, offering the reader tools to work with that span the spectrum of all the bodies and ultimately bring them into the subtle realms of cosmic ascension.

These tools are practical gems for the **purification, healing, cleansing, acceleration** and **ascension process** that cover the individual incarnated soul and extend into the vast monadic and cosmic realms.

DR. JOSHUA DAVID STONE

Dr. Stone has a Ph.D. in Transpersonal Psychology and is a licensed marriage, family and child counselor in Los Angeles, California. On a spiritual level, he anchors the Melchizedek Synthesis Light Academy & Ashram.

1 THE COMPLETE ASCENSION MANUAL

How to Achieve Ascension in This Lifetime
A synthesis of the past and guidance for ascension. An extraordinary compendium of practical techniques and spiritual history. Compiled from research and channeled information.
SOFTCOVER 297P.   ISBN 0-929385-55-1

2 SOUL PSYCHOLOGY

Keys to Ascension
Modern psychology deals exclusively with personality, ignoring the dimensions of spirit and soul. This book provides ground-breaking theories and techniques for healing and self-realization.
SOFTCOVER 256P.   ISBN 0-929385-56-X

3 BEYOND ASCENSION

How to Complete the Seven Levels of Initiation
Brings forth new channeled material that demystifies the 7 levels of initiation and how to attain them. It contains new information on how to open and anchor our 36 chakras.
SOFTCOVER 280P.   ISBN 0-929385-73-X

4 HIDDEN MYSTERIES

ETs, Ancient Mystery Schools and Ascension
Explores the unknown and suppressed aspects of Earth's past; reveals new information on the ET movement and secret teachings of the ancient mystery schools.
SOFTCOVER 330P.   ISBN 0-929385-57-8

5 THE ASCENDED MASTERS LIGHT THE WAY

Beacons of Ascension
The lives and teachings of 40 of the world's greatest saints and spiritual beacons provide a blueprint for total self-realization. Guidance from masters.
SOFTCOVER 258P.   ISBN 0-929385-58-6

6 COSMIC ASCENSION

Your Cosmic Map Home
Almost all the books on the planet on the subject of ascension are written about planetary ascension. Now, because of the extraordinary times in which we live, cosmic ascension is available here on Earth! Learn about self-realization, evolvement of nations and more.
SOFTCOVER 263P.   ISBN 0-929385-99-3

7 A BEGINNER'S GUIDE TO THE PATH OF ASCENSION
with REV. JANNA SHELLY PARKER

This volume covers the basics of ascension clearly and completely, from the spiritual hierarchy to the angels and star beings.
SOFTCOVER 166P.   ISBN 1-891824-02-3

8 GOLDEN KEYS TO ASCENSION AND HEALI

Revelations of Sai Baba and the Ascended Masters
This book represents the wisdom of the ascended mas densed into concise keys that serve as a spiritual guide. T golden keys present the multitude of insights Dr. S gleaned from his own background and his path to God-re
SOFTCOVER 205P.   ISBN 1-89

9 MANUAL FOR PLANETARY LEADERSHIP

Here at last is an indispensable book that has been urgen ed in these uncertain times, laying out the guidelines fo ship in the world and in one's life. It serves as a reference for moral and spiritual living.
SOFTCOVER 283P.   ISBN 1-891

10 YOUR ASCENSION MISSION

Embracing Your Puzzle Piece
with REV. JANNA SHELLEY PARKER
This book shows how each person's puzzle piece is jus and necessary as any other. Includes all aspects of living t expression of your individuality.
SOFTCOVER 249P.   ISBN 1-89

11 REVELATIONS OF A MELCHIZEDEK INITIATE

Dr. Stone's spiritual autobiography, beginning with his as initiation and progression into the 12th initiation. Fill insights, tools and information.
SOFTCOVER 306P.   ISBN 1-89

12 HOW TO TEACH ASCENSION CLASSES

This book serves as an ideal foundation for teaching a classes and presenting workshops. It covers an entire one year program of classes.
SOFTCOVER 135P.   ISBN 1-89

13 ASCENSION AND ROMANTIC RELATIONSHIP
with REV. JANNA SHELLEY PARKER
Inspired by Djwhal Khul, Dr. Stone has written a uniq about relationships from the perspective of the soul an rather than just the personality. This presents a broad p the problems and common traps of romantic relations offers much deep advice.
SOFTCOVER 184P.   ISBN 1-89

14 ASCENSION COMPLETE INDEX

Ascension Names and Ascended Master Terms Glossary complete index of all thirteen books.   ISBN 1-891

LIGHT TECHNOLOGY PUBLISHING
P.O. Box 3540 • Flagstaff, AZ

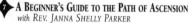

SONG OF FREEDOM

My Journey from the Abyss by Judith Moore

Judith Moore knew she'd been sick a lot more than most people—but it wasn't until she joined an incest survivors' group to help one of her adopted daughters that the memories began surfacing.

At first she feared for her sanity, for these recollections were of painful medical experiments, torture and sensory deprivation at the hands of the United States government.

In this brave and groundbreaking work, Judith Moore shares her shattering revelations of the reality of **HIGH-LEVEL MIND CONTROL**. She opens the pages of her journal and the innermost feelings of her heart to share with the reader her **JOURNEY TO WHOLENESS** and to healing. As memories flood her consciousness, she struggles to make sense of what is happening, to process the information in accordance with her lifelong worldview of love, intellectual curiosity and deep respect for nature.

Her early environment, rich in **NATIVE AMERICAN FOLKLORE**, helps her in her quest. She researches, travels, investigates and meditates in an effort to set herself free, to reclaim her very sense of herself as a person. Her search leads her into terrifying unknown territory and **ILLUMINATING DISCOVERIES** about her own psyche and that of today's society as a whole. $**19.95**

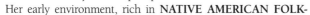

JUDITH'S MEMORIES BEGAN TO BRING TO THE SURFACE

- **PAINFUL MEDICAL EXPERIMENTS**
- **TORTURE**
- **SENSORY DEPRIVATION**
- **HIGH-LEVEL MIND CONTROL**

AT THE HANDS OF THE UNITED STATES GOVERNMENT!

Song of Freedom is a wake-up call to Western civilization! Moore's gripping account of her extraordinary life takes us to extremes of human experience—from depravity beyond comprehension to the triumph of one child's unassailable spirit. Song of Freedom dares us to take off the blinders we wear to what lies buried in our societal closets. Those who dare to look are taken on a transformational journey through the horrors of mind control and ritual abuse to Judith's amazing experiences of healing. The book is strewn with insights and gems of wisdom which prove that although fear often seems to have the upper hand, it is always love that triumphs in the end.

CHRYSTINE OKSANA, AUTHOR
Safe Passage to Healing: A Guide for Survivors of Ritual Abuse

JUDITH K. MOORE No longer a victim, Judith Moore now leads a productive life, teaching, sharing and channeling the truths that helped her in her journey to freedom.

LIGHT TECHNOLOGY PUBLISHING
P.O. BOX 3540 • FLAGSTAFF • AZ 86003
PHONE: (928) 526-1345
1-800-450-0985
FAX: (928) 714-1132
1-800-393-7017
www.lighttechnology.com

SEDONA

Journal of EMERGENCE!

Rated Number One!

We Offer Answers to Satisfy the Heart and to Inspire Lives!

The *Sedona Journal of Emergence* is the one monthly magazine readers never throw away. It features Predictables that discuss what's happening right now, this day, this month, and how you can make the most of the potentials created by the acceleration of frequency in your life on every level—physical, mental, emotional, spiritual— and on the integrated levels of wholeness that are becoming possibilities now.

It even offers your very own personal horoscope for each week of the month. No other monthly magazine offers the quantity and quality of guidance by other-dimensional beings to not only help you through these unprecedented times, but to help you make sense of and understand what all of this opening and expansion means to you!

It also contains the latest channeled information on what to do, as humans and the Earth move from the third to the fourth dimension, and reveals how these energies affect you and the Earth.

The *Sedona Journal* is filled with practical articles and features on New Age humor, healing, children's stories, ETs, UFOs, herbs, numerology, reincarnation and more!

Get SPECIAL UPDATES of channeled material before their on the web site with ELECTRONIC SUBSCRIPTIONS!

ELECTRON SUBSCRIPTIC available for S

Beginning is December 15, 2 for the January 2 issue.

$43⁰⁰/YEAR fo months anywhe on the planet!

Get the latest ch neling and astro 2 weeks before available on the newsstand.

Available in:
• Adobe Acrobat
• Microsoft Word slower modem